Wilmington:

Lost But Not Forgotten

The companion book to the popular lecture series first presented to the Historic Wilmington Foundation

by

Beverly Tetterton

Dram Tree Books

Books

A JEF Publications Company

First Edition 2005

Published in the United States of America by Dram Tree Books,
a JEF Publications company.

Publisher's Cataloging-in-Publication Data
(Provided by DRT Press)

Tetterton, Beverly
    Wilmington : lost but not forgotten / by Beverly Tetterton.
    p. cm.
    Includes bibliographical references and index.
    ISBN: 0-9723240-3-8

1. Architecture--Wilmington Region (N.C.). 2. Wilmington Region (N.C.)--History. 3. Cape Fear River (N.C.)--History. 4. Wrightsville Beach (N.C.)--History. 5. Kure Beach (N.C.)--History. 6. Carolina Beach (N.C.)--History. I. Title.

F254 .T48 W55 2005
975.6--dc22

10 9 8 7 6 5 4 3 2

Dram Tree Books
2801 Lyndon Avenue
Wilmington, N.C. 28405-3045
(910) 538-4076
dramtreebooks@ec.rr.com

*Discounts available
for educators.
Call or e-mail for terms.*

Dedication

This book is dedicated to

Edward F. Turberg

architectural historian, preservationist and friend.

Acknowledgements

I am indebted to the wonderful local history and photograph collections at the New Hanover County Public Library. I sincerely appreciate and am grateful for assistance from GlennTetterton, Joseph Sheppard, Michael Whaley, Marie Spencer, Elaine Henson, Jack Fryar, Tim Bottoms, Ed Turberg, J. Kenneth Davis, Harry Thornton, Randy Allen, Walter Conser, Madeline Flagler, Bob Cooke, W. B. Creasy, Carlton Allegood, Eric Kozen, Nancy Beeler, Janet Seapker, Susan Block, Sue Boney Ives, Gareth Evans and all of my fellow preservationists at the Historic Wilmington Foundation. I am especially appreciative for assistance from Ann Hewlett Hutteman. The last chapter is more hers than mine.

The Wilmington Riverfront

This aerial view reflects a compact city on the river in 1933, with quick residential access by foot or streetcar. At the time this photograph was taken the city looked to the river and the adjacent business district for its economic livelihood. The image reflects the apex of city living that had developed during the previous two hundred years.

Introduction

This publication grew out of a series of programs, which were prepared for the Historic Wilmington Foundation about buildings in Wilmington that had been torn down. As New Hanover County TV began to film the programs, the broadcasts became popular with a wide audience. The scope of the programs expanded to include "lost" businesses and industries with lectures for the Wilmington Rotary and Kiwanis clubs. Likewise, the repertoire increased with a lecture for the Wilmington Railroad Museum, which explained how and why the various railroads changed the city streetscape as well as how the loss of the Atlantic Coast Line Railroad precipitated urban renewal. Special attention was given to preservation efforts, which have afforded the city its many remaining architecturally significant buildings and neighborhoods.

According to the Julian calendar, Wilmington, North Carolina, was incorporated in 1739. Located on the east bank of the Cape Fear River, the original town is 28 nautical miles from the Atlantic Ocean. Built on several rises, more like sand dunes than hills, the town ascends 50 feet from the river shoreline. Despite navigational difficulties along the river, the town grew to become the largest city in the state before the Civil War. It remained so until the second decade of the 20th century, when the state's Piedmont tobacco and textile towns rose to prominence.

Wilmington's historical significance is reflected in the variety of architectural styles, streetscapes and in other aspects of its material culture. The Colonial town is most visible in the original grid pattern of the streets, the numbered streets running from north to south and the named streets running from east to west. Several periods of rapid growth have altered the city's passage through time. Very few buildings remain from the early town because of large fires and antebellum growth stimulated by the 1840 opening of the railroad.

Three other periods of sustained growth are also noteworthy. Recovery from the Civil War with increased port and rail expansion precipitated substantial commercial activity in the late nineteenth and early twentieth centuries. Increased business and industry, particularly of cotton and fertilizer, provided a new building boom both commercially and residentially, including moves to the first suburbs. This economic activity spread across the region, evident most noticeably in the development of nearby beaches. After a period of decline during the Great Depression, Wilmington experienced another burst of growth during World War II. Military facilities and the North Carolina Shipbuilding Company brought an unprecedented number of new residents who needed housing as well as a myriad of businesses to support their daily lives. The most recent growth came in the 1990s, after Wilmington was connected to the rest of country by Interstate Highway 40. The area, especially the beaches and rural sections of New Hanover County, became unrecognizable to former residents or visitors, who have been absent for the past twenty years.

Other external forces changed the landscape immeasurably. The loss of population and the destruction of the enormous railroad complex after the Atlantic Coast Line Railroad relocated its headquarters to Jacksonville, Florida, was a major blow to the economy of the city. Urban renewal was equally devastating to the historic waterfront.

This book provides an overview of Wilmington's historical landscape and the loss of many architectural and cultural treasures. New Hanover County, the smallest county in total area (land and water), and the county's incorporated towns have been included in this portrait. The region is so interconnected that the future of all is one and the same. Wilmington enters the twenty-first century at a time of critical decision: how much of the architectural heritage can be sacrificed in the interest of growth and development, without losing the very features which make Wilmington such a charming place to live or visit? How much of our material culture should we pass on to future generations? Finally, it is worth remembering how much we have lost, as well as what great riches continue to need our protection and preservation.

Beverly Tetterton
October, 2005

 Contents

Part One

City Living

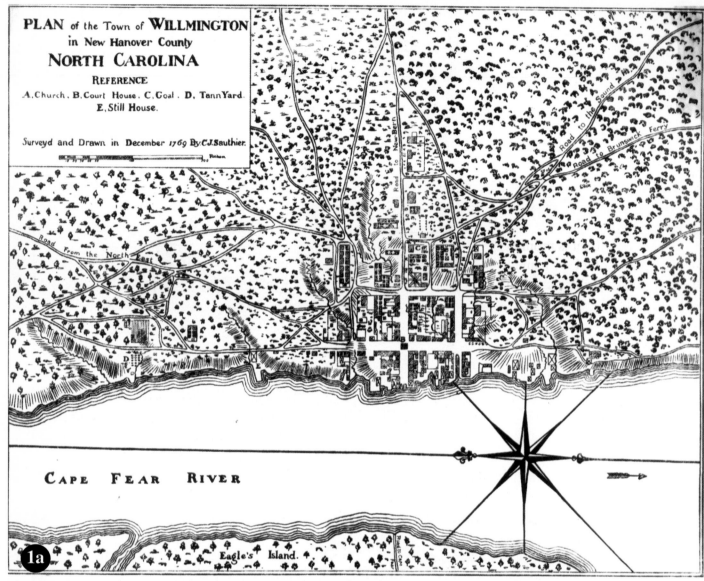

Wilmington in 1769, from the map drawn by C.J. Sauthier.

Colonial Wilmington

Wilmington was founded in 1733 and incorporated in 1739-1740. Although the town was laid out in a grid pattern and town lots sold accordingly, the Sauthier map and McKoy model suggest that residents took a more casual view of development. Buildings, dependencies and gardens encroached on neighbors. Elizabeth McKoy, who enthusiastically studied old New Hanover County deeds, created the model. Miss McKoy's depiction of Wilmington in 1771 was based on her extensive research on Wilmington land conveyances and the C.J. Sauthier map, surveyed and drawn in 1769.

The Sauthier map is the only contemporary source that allows an eighteenth century glimpse of the town. It also shows topographical features, particularly streams and wetlands that no one living today can remember or imagine amidst the current asphalt, brick and concrete landscape. City streets evolved from what appear to be haphazard paths leading out of the village in all directions. As early as 1749, residents of Wilmington were constructing underground tunnels to divert the numerous streams that ran throughout the town. It took many years to harness the streams and paths into perfect city blocks and straight tree-lined streets. In 1795, the town began filling in the inlets and wetlands along the waterfront to form Water Street. The early Dock Street inlet was large enough for vessels to moor there.

Covering only a few of today's city blocks, the map and the model are reminiscent of a time when it was important for town dwellers to live and work as close to the waterfront as possible. The Colonial port was located in the area surrounding the foot of Market Street. Miss McKoy's model illustrates the wooden wharves and warehouses lining the banks of the Cape Fear River.

Market Street is prominent in both views. It took its name from the town market, which can be seen in the model as the building in the middle of the street closest to the water. Moving east from the river, the next large building is the eighteenth century New Hanover

Tunnels of Jacob's Run beneath downtown Wilmington in 1972.

County Courthouse. During the Colonial period, this courthouse serviced much of southeastern North Carolina. East of the courthouse was the combined town hall and a second market. At the eastern end of the model and the map is St. James Church, which was consecrated in 1770.

The map and the model are also important because they show the location and size of the town's building stock. Brick was the predominant building material for the church, courthouse, market, and a few other

Elizabeth McKoy's model of Colonial Wilmington.

structures. Brick was important to the fledgling town because the original charter hinged on the addition of eight brick buildings within a period of two years after incorporation. However, the majority of houses, warehouses, and dependencies were constructed with wood. The surrounding longleaf pine forests provided an ample supply of wood products for construction. The number of residences seems minimal but it must be remembered that very few people actually lived in town in the eighteenth century. Inn-keepers and tavern-keepers, tradesmen, merchants and a few professionals lived in Wilmington full-time. Otherwise, many of the dwellings were townhouses, owned by county landowners. Full town capacity occurred four times a year when the county court was in session. The Burgwin-Wright House, built in 1770, is a good example of an eighteenth century townhouse. The dwelling, which still stands, can be seen on the model at the southwest corner of Third and Market streets.

Wilmington's central business district in 1855.

Market Street in 1855

In 1855, a sketch artist for *Ballou's Pictorial Drawing-Room Companion* captured Market Street looking from Second Street toward the river. These blocks of Market Street comprised a majority of the town's central business district. Two large fires, in 1840 and 1845, had previously destroyed most of the buildings between Dock and Princess streets. The two and three-story brick buildings shown in the sketch were more substantial fireproof replacements.

According to the article, the Carolina Hotel, seen on the far right of the drawing, was the premier place to stay while in town on business. The Gothic Revival-style building next to the hotel was St. John's Masonic Lodge, built in 1841. The Masons rented the ground floor storefronts and their lodge rooms were located in the upper floors. In the distance the masts of several sailing ships can be seen along the waterfront. An auction is being held at the city market (built 1848), located in the middle of the intersection of Front and Market streets.

The article states that, "the wagons, driven by slaves, contained produce brought into town from the surrounding farms." The large pole near Front and Water streets was the telegraph connection to the city. The streets, which consisted of nothing more than hard packed dirt, were often muddy. Sidewalks were elevated from the street and made of wood. The town had streetlights in 1855. There is one, barely visible in the sketch, at the corner of Market and North Second streets.

Very few pre-Civil War buildings remain on this section of Market Street. St. John's Masonic Lodge (125-127 Market Street), the Dawson Building (19 Market Street), and the River Boat Landing Restaurant (SE corner of Water and Market streets), although greatly altered, still exist.

South Front Street, looking north in February 1865, after the city fell to Union troops.

Wilmington in 1865

The 1865 sketch of Wilmington, taken from *Frank Leslie's Illustrated Newspaper*, is important because it is the only known contemporary view of the city at the time of the Civil War. Federal officials took photographs of New Bern and other towns that fell early in the war; however, Wilmington was one of the last to fall to Union forces. If Confederates or blockade-runners photographed Wilmington, their work is yet to be discovered.

Although the sketch was drawn somewhat out of perspective, the artist revealed much about the city at a critical time in its history. The artist's main focus was on prisoners marching along South Front Street. After Wilmington was occupied on February 22, 1865, the city became overcrowded with thousands of recently freed Union prisoners of war, Confederate captives and refugees.

The drawing shows a mixture of wood-frame and brick buildings. The town's crowning pre-Civil War architectural achievement, City Hall/Thalian Hall (1855-58), is seen on the skyline at the upper right corner of the sketch. The U.S. Custom House (1844) is shown on the waterfront with a small number 3 written above it. The large brick building south of the Custom House is the three-story ice house. In the center of the sketch is a white two and one-half-story wood-frame building. It was previously Ann Quince's Tavern, where George Washington was entertained during his 1781 visit to Wilmington. The building escaped several fires, only to be torn down in the 1920s. In 1865, wood-frame houses with cypress shake shingles, side yards or back gardens, and picket fences were still commonplace in the center of the city.

A view of Market Street, looking west from near Third Street, circa 1910.

Market Street West

From Second Street to Fifth Avenue, Market Street had a mixture of commercial and residential buildings. The postcard view on the opposite page shows the north side of Market Street from the intersection of Third and Market. To the right of the image is the Dr. Armand deRosset House. Constructed in the late eighteenth or early nineteenth century, the three-story dwelling reflected the good taste and success of one of the few town physicians. When the house was built, the second story porch provided a good view of the river. The kitchen and other dependencies were located behind the house on Third Street. A tall fence, that had a door instead of a gate, shielded the outbuildings from the street. Market Street's gentle slope toward the river is reflected in the construction of the front porch. During the Civil War, the deRossets vacated the house and it was used as the district headquarters for the Confederate Army. By 1905, when the postcard view was taken, commercial buildings were encroaching on the old house. It was torn down in 1919 and replaced by a Standard Oil Company filling station and repair service.

The postcard image above shows Market Street two lots west of the intersection with Third Street. To the left is a one-story Italianate-style commercial building. Huge brackets support the flat roof. The arched door and windows, that cover most of the facade, rival those at City Hall. A recreation of this building, a favorite of architectural historians, would be a great addition to Wilmington's twenty-first century landscape. Over time, offices, small businesses and car lots occupied the property. It was torn down circa 1951.

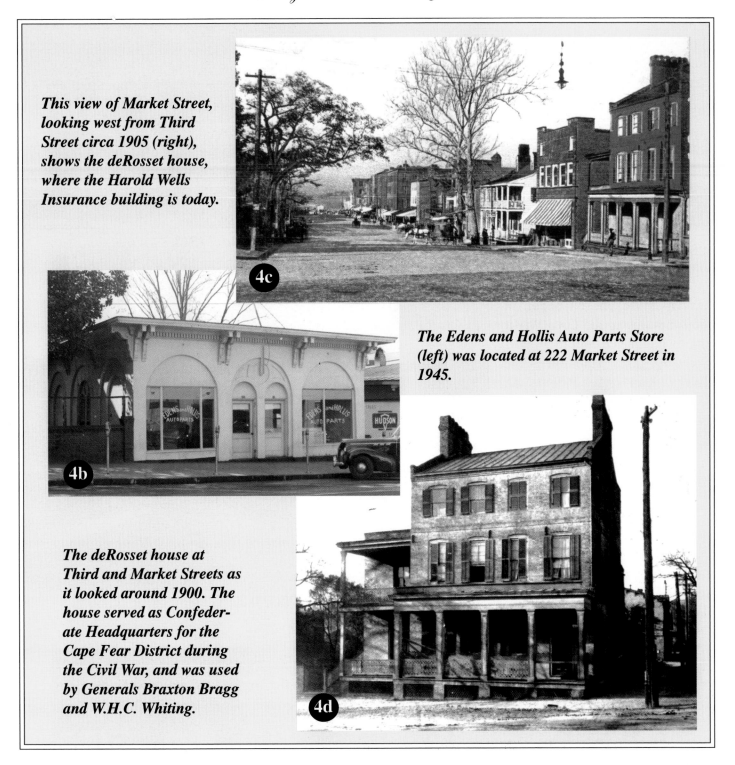

This view of Market Street, looking west from Third Street circa 1905 (right), shows the deRosset house, where the Harold Wells Insurance building is today.

4c

The Edens and Hollis Auto Parts Store (left) was located at 222 Market Street in 1945.

4b

The deRosset house at Third and Market Streets as it looked around 1900. The house served as Confederate Headquarters for the Cape Fear District during the Civil War, and was used by Generals Braxton Bragg and W.H.C. Whiting.

4d

Market Street East

When Wilmington was incorporated in 1739-1740 Boundary Street (Fifth Avenue) was the eastern perimeter of the town. As the city grew, Market Street, east of Fifth developed as a mostly residential street. East of Third Street, Market became a boulevard with a tree-lined plaza. Wealthy citizens built grand and architecturally significant houses there. The trend to build large and fashionable homes on Market Street continued with the development of the streetcar suburbs.

In 1859-1860, Dr. John D. Bellamy built his remarkable columned mansion on the northeast corner of Fifth and Market streets. It symbolized the opulence and elegance of living on east Market Street. The postcard image

Market Street, looking east from Fifth Avenue, around 1915.

depicts Market Street looking from the Bellamy Mansion toward St. Paul's Lutheran Church.

Construction of the Gothic Revival style church began in 1859, but due to the Civil War it was not completed until 1869. Next to the Bellamy Mansion is the Queen Ann-style Robert R. Bellamy House, which burned in the early 1980s.

In 2005, only nine houses from Fifth Avenue to Twelfth Street survive. Most of them are no longer residences. However, landscaping on Market Street improved in the 1990s, when city councilman J.D. Causey persuaded the city to bury the electric lines and plant new trees and shrubs in the plaza and along the sidewalks.

Market Street, looking east from Seventh Street, in 1910.

Market Street, looking west from Eighth Street, in 1910.

Third Street, looking north from Chestnut Street, circa 1930.

Third Street

Wilmington experienced a tremendous building boom after the railroad was completed in 1840. Simultaneously, Third Street became an affluent residential street, populated by well-to-do merchants and industrialists. Many large houses, built in the latest architectural style, were constructed along Third Street prior to the Civil War.

During the nineteenth century the majority of buildings on both North and South Third streets were dwellings. Three Gothic Revival-style churches (First Presbyterian, St. James and St. John's) and two government buildings (New Hanover County Courthouse and City Hall) were among the few non-residences on the street. All of the structures were built close to the street.

Market, Fifth and Third streets were intended to be boulevards and are ninety-nine feet wide, or thirty-three feet wider than other city streets. South Third Street had a twenty-five foot plaza, room enough for a double row of

Third Street, looking north from Orange Street, in 1910.

Third Street, looking north from near Orange Street, in 1910.

trees. Granite curbing and brick-pavers were laid about 1905. When automobile traffic demanded more street space, the plazas were narrowed to ten feet. The original plazas can still be viewed across the railroad cut on North Fifth Avenue. The wide plaza did not exist on Third Street from Market Street to the railroad cut.

*Third Street, South from Ann Street,
Wilmington, N. C.*

6a

*The Live Oaks that have
provided shade on one of
Wilmington's best traveled
thoroughfares were first
planted in the 1870s.*

The Kenan Fountain
Market Street & Fifth Avenue

An architectural gem, the Kenan Memorial Fountain was erected in 1921 in the middle of the large intersection of Fifth Avenue and Market Street. Wilmington native, William Rand Kenan, Jr., gave the fountain to the city to memorialize his parents, William Rand and Mary Hargrave Kenan. Carrere and Hastings of New York, a respected architectural firm that designed the New York Public Library, drew the plans for the fountain. It was made out of Indiana limestone and cost $43,000. The fountain was sculpted in New York, then dismantled and shipped to Wilmington where it was rebuilt. The postcard view reveals the picturesque location of the fountain at a time when both Market Street and Fifth Avenue retained their wide plazas.

When Mr. Kenan gave the fountain to the city most residents still walked or took the streetcar. However, some pessimistic citizens predicted that it would become a traffic hazard. Their forecast came true as the city grew and automobiles became a preferred mode of transportation. In 1953, the North Carolina Highway Safety Commission recommended that the fountain be moved to a safer location. Kenan and others took the opposite view, that the fountain actually reduced speeding. A compromise was reached when stoplights were installed, the streets widened to two lanes and the fountain reduced in size. North Carolina traffic engineers brought up the removal of the fountain again in 1969. Architect Leslie N. Boney, Jr., defended the fountain, saying he did

7a

Kenan Fountain, at the intersection of Fifth Avenue and Market Street, circa 1930.

A 1930 view of the Kenan Fountain that shows some of the large houses that existed at the intersection of Fifth Avenue and Market Street.

not know of a single other city in North Carolina with a monument and fountain to compare with the Kenan Fountain. "It's just part of the civic scene," he said, "people go all the way to Europe to see fountains of this type." The traffic engineers backed off and a second reprieve was granted.

Over the ensuing years the Kenan Fountain fell into disrepair several times and the city felt it was too expensive to repair and maintain. It often sat neglected until 1977 when the Historic Wilmington Foundation and the Residents of Old Wilmington donated funds to repair it and activate the water again. The Residents contributed plants and continued to water them for many years. Despite recurring traffic accidents and occasional pranksters who delight in putting soap or dye in the fountain, the City of Wilmington became fully committed to maintaining and preserving the fountain that was almost lost. Extensive repairs were completed in April, 2005, and the old landmark was proudly rededicated.

It is rare to find an image of the Kenan Fountain taken from the northwest corner of Fifth and Market. Most photographers probably preferred the Bellamy Mansion as a backdrop. The postcard image shows the large houses built on the southeast corner of the intersection. On the corner facing Market was the Italianate-style John Dawson House. It was constructed in 1857-58, one year before the Bellamy Mansion. The Dawson lot measured 132 feet on Fifth and 82 1/2 feet on Market. It was large enough to have room for a formal garden in the side yard and several outbuildings in the rear yard. Irish-born John Dawson was a successful dry goods merchant and a stockholder in the Wilmington and Weldon Railroad. He was magistrate of police and a two-time mayor of Wilmington. The house was torn down circa 1962.

Streets, Granite Curbing, Sidewalks and Retaining Walls

The first paving materials in Wilmington were ballast stones. Conveniently discarded by departing vessels, the endless supply of stone was also used for house foundations, retaining walls and filler when Water Street was created out of the marshy waterfront. As late as the 1980s, ballast stones were still fairly easy to find lying around the downtown. Several ballast stone retaining walls survive. A good example can be seen behind the Mitchell-Anderson House at 102 Orange Street.

8c

8e

Brick streets and granite curbing at Third and Princess streets in 1910 (left), and a concrete block sidewalk at the corner of Dock Street and Fifth Avenue in 1968 (above).

Belgian paving stones (rectangular blocks of quarried stone or granite) were used to pave streets in the later part of the nineteenth century. They were also used as ballast during the time of wooden sailing ships. Many of them were discarded during urban renewal and others have been paved over with asphalt. The late historian, Bill Reaves, lamented in a 1975 newspaper article that the city had removed the old block from Lodge Alley and was using it to fill in the old boat slips on Water Street, rather than exhibit it in the historic district. Lodge Alley was an L-shaped alley that ran from the south side of Red Cross Street to Front Street. Old Belgian blocks can still be seen at Chandler's Wharf and in front of the Cotton Exchange.

In 1891, city officials began to flirt with the idea of brick roadways. The *Morning Star*, 13 December 1891, reported the following: "Bricks make practically a noiseless pavement; they fit so closely that there is no inter-spaces to retain filth and breed disease; a brick pavement is easily cleaned; it is easily repaired; bricks can be made of any size and shape for gutters, slopes, etc., without much, if any, additional cost; brick pavements are smooth and reduce the tractive power and wear and tear of vehicles almost to a minimum. Bricks do not polish under wear, and hence afford a good foothold to horses; they are not affected appreciably by moisture,

8a

Belgian block streets in downtown Wilmington, circa 1900.

frost or fire. The first cost of a brick pavement is less than any good pavement; hence on the score of health, comfort and cost brick pavements have much to commend them." By 1900, city workers were constantly laying brick pavement from the inner city outward. Businesses and residents were assessed for the cost of laying the brick in front of their buildings.

Preservationists have repeatedly worked to save Wilmington's old brick streets. The 1970s photograph shows historic district residents removing the seal coating that city workers had spread in preparation for pavement at the intersection of Fourth and Ann streets. They also hired a security guard to protect their efforts. As late as 1997, the controversy still raged. Advice from other historic cities, which envy Wilmington's miles of brick streets, convinced city officials to do their utmost to repair and save this important historic resource.

Wilmington paving bricks, which weigh about ten pounds, are marked with seals of their manufacturer—Peebles Block, Augusta Block, and Southern Clay.

Downtown residents work to preserve the neighborhood's distinctive brick streets in 1973.

Remaining Belgian block pavers from Lodge Alley in 1975.

Before sidewalks, residents had to dart back and forth to avoid mud holes and sinking sand. The first sidewalks were made of wooden planks that were raised six to eight inches above ground. Residential areas had a few wooden sidewalks, but were generally sand paths. Examples of sandy residential walkways can still be viewed south of Marstellar Street on both sides of Fourth Street and Fifth Avenue. In the late nineteenth century, brick sidewalks began replacing wooden ones. Here and there, an old brick sidewalk can still be seen in the residential area of the historic district. Good illustrations are located on the southeast and southwest corners of Sixth and Ann streets. Early on, some residents installed their own sidewalks. Octagonal cement block walks (c. 1900) are still visible on the northeast and northwest corners of Fifth Avenue and Dock Street. Concrete sidewalks were laid by the second and third decades of the twentieth century.

Retaining walls were constructed of stone, brick, and patent stone. Large numbers of these walls survive in the historic district, but many were destroyed on the north side during Urban Renewal. They continue to disappear as the north side experiences new development.

9a

The "Belt" streetcar line was the first to carry passengers around town. This photo was taken around 1915.

Streetcars & Beach Cars

Streetcars were the heart and soul of city living. Whether for business or pleasure, they provided a convenient way of getting around town. The Wilmington Street Railway Company was chartered in 1887. It began with horse drawn cars, which were shipped to Wilmington by steamboat from Brooklyn, New York. Initially, the company had twenty-nine horses. After four years of operation, tracks had been laid and the railway electrified. In the beginning, there were five miles of tracks. Called the "Belt" it ran from Princess Street south down Front Street to Castle Street, then east on Castle Street to Sixth Street, then north on Sixth Street to Orange Street, then east on Orange Street to Ninth Street, then north on Ninth Street to Princess Street, then west on Princess Street to Front, where the trip began again. Eventually other lines were built to connect other parts of town—North Fourth Street, Sunset Park, Carolina Place, Carolina Heights and Winter Park.

During the early decades of the twentieth century, these extended lines fostered an explosion of suburbs. The early cars were designed to be open in the summer in order to catch the breeze. They had canvas covers that could be pulled down in case of rainy weather. Winter cars were closed.

The advent of regular beach car service to Wrightsville Beach offered easy access to the general public.

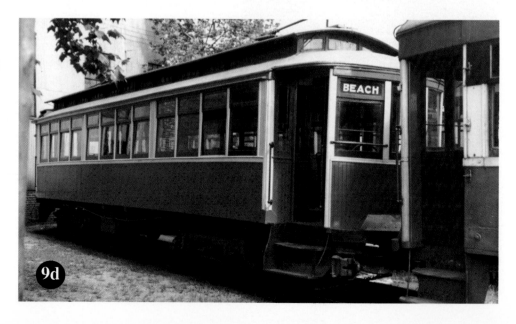

9d

The Beach Line was the most popular of all the lines because of its association with Wrightsville Beach. In 1902, after the consolidation of several railways, electric beach cars began to run to the beach. Within a few years they were highly acclaimed and created immense interest and development in the resort town.

In 1939, Wilmington was the last city in North Carolina to relinquish its street railway system. The beach cars discontinued operation in 1940.

Princess Street (right) was a mess when crews worked to lay the streetcar tracks in 1907. By 1910, passengers could ride the gleaming rails from Princess Street to Wrightsville Beach (below).

Pembroke Jones Playground, across from New Hanover High School, in 1930.

Carolina Heights & Winoca Terrace

Located north of Market Street, from Fourteenth Street to the National Cemetery, Carolina Heights and Winoca Terrace were among Wilmington's first suburbs. Living on the edge of the city became popular because it allowed residents to build new homes with up-to-date plumbing, electrical wiring, and modern conveniences without the added cost of demolishing an older structure in order to build. The streetcar made it possible to live in the suburbs and still rely on public transportation. From Princess Street, residents of Carolina Heights and Winoca Terrace could catch a streetcar downtown or a beach car out to Wrightsville Beach. The suburbs allowed middle-class people to build new houses in the latest architectural styles. They also gave wealthy people the opportunity to construct grand houses on large lots.

Most of the landscape and buildings in Carolina Heights and Winoca Terrace survive. However, the buildings on the south side of Market Street between Sixteenth and Seventeenth streets were torn down from 1951 to 1954 when a modern shopping center was constructed. Pembroke Jones Playground, a block west, has been reduced to a few tennis courts.

Carolina Heights, circa 1920.

In the mid-1990s, three houses were lost in the 1600 block of Princess Street. The St. Paul's Episcopal Church Rectory, located on the southeast corner of Sixteenth and Princess streets, was torn down and replaced by a playground. Neighborhood preservationists were alarmed when two other houses faced demolition to make way for a parking lot. The 1920s Joseph M. Block House, located at 1618 Princess Street was torn down despite the Historic District Commission's imposition of a 365-day delay to find an interested party to move it. Fortunately, the house next door was saved when it was moved to 411 Castle Street.

Princess and 17th Sts., Carolina Heights, @ilmington, N. C.

Another view of Carolina Heights, this one from 1918.

The Joseph M. Block house (left), a good example of the kind of houses found in the Carolina Heights and Winoca Terrace neighborhoods, as it was in 1995 just prior to its demolition that same year (below).

Part Two

Residences

The first house in Wilmington, drawn in 1855.

The First House in Wilmington
The William Hooper House

In 1855, when the sketch of the first house built in Wilmington was published in *Ballou's Pictorial Drawing-Room Companion*, the reporter described it as being located on a side street, north of Market. He said that, "within the space of a hundred years, it has become the nucleus of a considerable city." It was remarkable that the old structure had survived, especially when 200 buildings were destroyed during the fire of 1819.

This old house was in the same location as the one purchased by William Hooper in 1770. Hooper (1742-1790) was a native of Boston, Massachusetts. He studied at Harvard College before moving to Wilmington, in 1764, to practice law. In 1767, he married Anne Clark of New Hanover County, the daughter of a local planter. The Hoopers spent little time in their townhouse

A sketch of Declaration of Independence signer William Hooper's Wilmington house drawn in 1883.

because he traveled throughout the colony practicing law and politics, and she, more than likely, stayed with her family when he was gone. They also had a much larger residence, Finian, which overlooked Masonboro Sound. Attorney, orator, legislator, and patriotic leader, William Hooper is remembered as one of North Carolina's three signers of the Declaration of Independence.

Over the years, a second story was added to the little house and it became a dependency for a dwelling that faced North Second Street. Wilmington's first known attempt at historic preservation occurred in 1882 when the Second Street house and dependencies faced demolition. Col. Roger Moore asked if he could purchase the old building and have it moved to a more public place where its historical significance could be preserved. Unfortunately, he was unable to make the transaction, and it was torn down.

Cornelius Harnett's Maynard, in 1855. The city's Sweeny Water Plant sits on the land today.

Maynard & Hilton

Maynard was the name of the plantation house built for Cornelius Harnett (1772-1781), Revolutionary statesman. Built in 1750, the house faced the Cape Fear River from a high bluff on the north end of town. In 1855, when a sketch of this house was featured in *Ballou's Pictorial Drawing-Room Companion*, the reporter referred to Harnett as the "Samuel Adams of the South." He was responsible for raising troops, arming and equipping an army, and planning military tactics in North Carolina during the American Revolution. He also served for three years in the Continental Congress. In 1781, Major James Craig imprisoned Harnett during the British occupation of Wilmington. Suffering from poor health caused by his imprisonment, he died shortly after his release.

The side of Hilton facing away from the river in 1892.

In 1784, Maynard was sold to John Hill and renamed Hilton. Within a few years the property passed to William H. Hill (1767-1808), lawyer, legislator, congressmen, and planter. A founder of the University of North Carolina, he served on the first board of trustees from 1791 until his death.

The architectural style of Hilton was Georgian. The brick house had a beautiful Chinese Chippendale balustrade and atypical mansard roof. An attempt to preserve the significant structure occurred in the early 1890s, when a Baltimore lumber company bought the property and scheduled the house for demolition. The Wilmington Historical and Scientific Society lamented in an 1892 newspaper that, "This house was built in 1750, it is said, and today it is in a splendid state of preservation. The brick and material were brought from England and the walls of the house are still good, with the exception of one spot. In as much as this historical house is to be torn down, would it not be well for the city to purchase it and have it removed to a park or some other place where it can be preserved? If the city cannot purchase it, would it not be well for the citizens to purchase the old house and save it from demolition?" The pre-demolition photograph, taken in 1892, shows an intact building, a modern-day preservationist's dream project. Ironically, the Hilton property did become a park shortly after the plantation house was torn down. Hilton Park was a popular place for picnics and other social gatherings. Football, baseball and golf were played there. Today, the park is home to the World's Largest Living Christmas Tree and the Sweeney Water Plant.

Hilton's river side in 1892.

The Governor's Mansion

No other dwelling in Wilmington has been inhabited by such a variety of interesting occupants, who initiated architectural changes reflective of their personalities, tastes and the times. The name of this house was derived from its first owner, Edward Bishop Dudley (1789-1855). Born in Onslow County, he served as an officer of a regiment that guarded Wilmington during the War of 1812. He moved to Wilmington after the war and began a long career in politics. Dudley represented the Wilmington District in the North Carolina House of Commons twice, and was a one-term congressman. In 1836, he was elected Governor of North Carolina, the first elected by popular vote. During his two terms as Governor (1836-1840), the state witnessed the most progressive period in its anti-bellum history. Dudley's zeal to improve transportation within the state was evidenced by his enthusiasm for the Wilmington and Weldon Railroad. He used his political savvy to bring the railroad to Wilmington and was its first president. He chose one of the prettiest hills overlooking the Cape Fear River as the site for his house. Tradition says it was constructed as early as 1825. A house fire severely damaged the building in 1843. The vented frieze was probably added when Dudley had to replace the entire roof after the fire.

The Dudley Mansion when it was owned by James Sprunt in 1908.

The dwelling was occupied next by Dr. Sterling B. Everitt (1791-1855). It is not known if his widow, Amelia (1803-1873), lived there throughout the Civil War or sought refuge in another town. However, in the fall of 1864 she was living there when she advertised it for rent. Francis W. Kerchner (1829-1910), wholesale grocer, and his wife, Lydia Hatch Kerchner (1834-1894), had moved in by the early 1870s. During their tenancy they made improvements to the house. In 1885, they sold it to J. Pembroke Jones when they moved next door.

By 1890, the mansion at 400 South Front Street became the residence of wealthy rice mill owner and financier, J. Pembroke Jones (1859-1943). When another fire occurred in 1895, Jones and his wife, Sarah Green

The Dudley Mansion when it was owned by J. Laurence Sprunt in the 1930s.

Jones (1858-1919), went to live at Airlie, their summer estate. The earliest photograph of the house shows what it looked like during the Jones tenancy. The main body of the two-story dwelling was capped with a cupola and ended by one-story wings. A one-story porch extended across the central body of the house, and the porte cochere hid a second story balcony.

The next owners were James Sprunt (1846-1924), rice planter, cotton exporter and local historian; and wife, Luola Murchison Sprunt (1860-1916). The style of the house changed dramatically in 1895, when they raised the wings to two stories and added an enormous Corinthian portico. The cupola was removed, the roof changed, and the eaves adorned to match the portico. The new Neoclassical Revival-style facade exemplified prominence and importance when President William Howard Taft was invited to breakfast there during his 1909 visit to Wilmington.

By 1924, the house had passed on to J. Laurence Sprunt (1883-1973), vice-president of Alexander Sprunt and Sons, cotton exporters. He removed the portico and front porch, and gave the dwelling a Colonial Revival-style presence.

The Dudley Mansion when owned by Pembroke Jones in the 1890s (right), and when it was an Elks Lodge in 1949 (above).

In 1945, the building became the clubhouse for Wilmington Lodge No. 532 of the Elks. They placed a large metal Elks head on the facade over the central second floor window.

Thomas H. Wright, Jr., and wife, Elizabeth, purchased the house in 1969. Three years later the Wrights allowed the Historic Wilmington Foundation to make the building its headquarters, rent-free. Mr. Wright was an organizing member of the Foundation and its first president. An ardent preservationist, he provided leadership and financial support during the early years of the organization. In 1985, when the Foundation moved its headquarters, the Dudley Mansion was placed in the hands of the Wright's son, Thomas H. Wright III, who undertook a meticulous renovation and restoration. Preservationists thought that the old house was saved forever. After Thomas Wright III sold the mansion, it changed hands a few times. Unfortunately, an illegal land transfer in 2003 put the mansion again in jeopardy. Unoccupied, it began to decline. In 2005, preservationists were relieved when a new owner, sensitive to the historical and architectural significance of the building, purchased the 170-year-old mansion.

The Brickhouse House, circa 1890.

Brickhouse House

The Brickhouse residence, located on the southwest corner of Front and Church streets, was built in the early nineteenth century. After Capt. Nathan E. Brickhouse (1800-1869) died unexpectedly from complications involving a sawmill work accident, his estate was not settled for nearly twenty years. The long drawn out settlement was probably the reason why the old house stood until the 1890s. It is reminiscent of early houses that extended into the street.

The Potter House as it looked in 1908 (below), and as it looked circa 1928 (left).

Captain Samuel Potter House

The Captain Samuel Potter House looks as though it may be the same colonial two-story wood-frame structure as seen on the Sauthier map and McKoy model (see page 3). The 1920s photograph shows Georgian-style elements- a symmetrical layout of the building, six over six-pane windows, and an engaged two-tier piazza with simple posts and railings. By the 1840s, the building was owned by Captain Samuel Potter, who entertained Henry Clay when he visited Wilmington in April, 1844. The nationally known legislator and orator spoke to a large crowd from the second-story porch. Captain Potter may have remodeled the old house, because during Clay's visit a newspaper reported that the house was "new and commodious." By the 1860s, the house was occupied by Dr. Francis W. Potter, Confederate surgeon, and wife Mary Hyde Potter.

Dr Potter was the superintendent of health. He also had a great interest in botany. Upon his death, his widow donated his large collection of botanical books to the University of North Carolina. They can still be used at the university's extensive botany library. Mrs. Potter outlived her husband by thirty-five years. The old house, which was located at 221 Market Street, was torn down in 1928 when the Chipley Universal Motor Company purchased it. Later, Cape Fear Ford occupied the property for many years.

Dr. Cranmer House

The Dr. John B. Cranmer (1874-1954) House was located at 311 Market Street. The white two-story, wood-frame dwelling was built in 1831 as the rectory for St. James Episcopal Church. The Federal style structure is reminiscent of similar dwellings in the coastal towns of Beaufort, Swansboro and Southport. From 1919 to 1954, it was the home of Dr. Cranmer, the Chairman of the New Hanover Board of Health and President of the New Hanover Medical Society. He practiced medicine in Wilmington for forty-nine years. The Cranmer house was torn down in 1956.

The Dr. Cranmer House around 1930.

16a

Hill-Wright-Wootten House

The Hill-Wright-Wootten House was built in the late eighteenth or early nineteenth century. Located at Eleven South Third Street, the two and one half-story Federal-style dwelling was built over a raised basement. The porches were massive and handsomely decorated with dentil molding, beautiful columns and an unusual balustrade. The house is reminiscent of early townhouses that protruded into streets that were less defined than today. Before air conditioning, the front porch constituted a well-used extra room of the house. The dwelling was constructed for Dr. John Hill. His daughter, Eliza Ann, married William Augustus Wright in 1830, and the dwelling became their residence.

In 1903, an Episcopal minister, the Rev. Edward Wootten, and his wife, Eliza Jewett, acquired the property. It remained in the Wootten family until St. James Episcopal Church purchased it in 1952. The house was torn down in 1955 when Milton Hall was constructed.

17a

17b

The Hill-Wright-Wootten House in 1905 (above), and as it looked in the 1950s (right).

The Sorosis Club House in the 1920s (left).

The same Sorosis Club House in 1955 (above).

Sorosis Club House

To the north of City Hall was the Shadrack M. West House (circa 1858), a large three-story Italianate dwelling that featured a belvedere on the roof. The North Carolina Sorosis bought the property from the West heirs in 1914. The North Carolina Sorosis was organized in 1895 and is the oldest federated women's club in the state. The name was chosen for a similar club in New York City and is a Greek botanical term for "a cluster of flowers on a stem." The club remodeled the West house by bricking the exterior and shortening the front porch. Clubrooms were on the first floor; the second and third floors contained rental units. In the mid-1960s, the club sold the building to the City of Wilmington. It was demolished in 1967 and the property turned into a parking lot.

The Edward Kidder House, a grand antebellum residence.

Edward Kidder House

The Edward Kidder House was located at 101 South Third Street. Edward Kidder (1805-1855) moved to Wilmington from Massachusetts about 1826. By the early 1840s, when he built his large residence, he was married to Ann Potter and was a successful lumber merchant. One of the grandest of Wilmington's pre-Civil War dwellings, the three-story, five-bay frame house was located near the southeast corner of Third and Dock streets. The original property encompassed two full lots on Third Street, which ran all the way to Fourth Street. The rear yard had numerous outbuildings, including a kitchen, laundry, servant quarters, and stables. Side yards contained gardens and a greenhouse. The house burned about 1965.

20a

The Kenan House as it looked in the 1920s.

Kenan House

About 1852, Levi A. Hart built a large house on the northwest corner of Third Street and Cottage Lane. The two-story, wood-frame Italianate-style dwelling was designed by architect, James F. Post. Two structures remain from the complex of outbuildings that stood behind the house: the Hart Carriage House and the Wine House. Levi Hart (1809-1883) was a partner in Hart & Bailey Iron Works. The cast-iron fence, made at his shop, can still be seen on Third Street.

About 1915, the house was purchased by Annie Hill Kenan (1852-1950), widow of James Graham Kenan (1839-1912). Mrs. Kenan, her daughter Emily (1875-1963), and son Owen (1872-1964), lived at 111 South Third Street for many years. They enlarged the porch and added a massive two-story Neoclassical Revival-style portico. A parking lot replaced the house in 1965.

Greek Revival-Style Townhouses

Wilmington's mid-nineteenth century prosperity was apparent in the construction of grand Greek Revival-style townhouses. This style of architecture was very popular in North Carolina from the 1830s until the Civil War. It embraced the architectural forms of ancient Greece and was characterized by symmetrical flat surfaces and engaged porticos supported by heavy pillars or columns.

21a

The P.K. Dickinson House as it looked in 1865, is a fine example of Wilmington's Greek Revival-style townhouses.

Wilmington townhouses characteristically had large lots with plenty of room for outbuildings and gardens. Mrs. William "Daisy" Lamb, wife of the commanding officer of Fort Fisher, wrote in 1861, "the streets of the city are wide and the houses are all separate and have very pretty gardens around them."

A terrible fire on April 30, 1843 destroyed the northern part of town from Princess Street between Second and Water streets. In two hours, from the time the alarm was given, the fire had reached the Railroad Depot. No more than a dozen buildings were left standing. The loss was estimated at $300,000. The fire consumed 27 houses, 45 businesses, the Custom House, Front Street Methodist Church and all of the railroad buildings. The town was, according to the newspaper, left *destitute*. On the other hand, the fire presented a grand opportunity to rebuild a new downtown. Several homeowners rebuilt in the popular Greek Revival-style. Unfortunately, none of these large residences on North Front Street survive. They were demolished and replaced by commercial buildings during a building boom around the turn of the twentieth century.

P.K. Dickinson House

The P. K. Dickinson House, located on the northeast corner of Front and Chestnut streets, was equal to houses of the same period that can still be seen in Richmond or Savannah. Early in the nineteenth century, Platt K. Dickinson (1794-1867)

22a

The P.K. Dickinson House as it looked in the 1890s.

moved from New England to Wilmington and founded a profitable lumber business. In the 1830s, he enthusiastically supported bringing the railroad to the Port City and served on the board of the Wilmington and Weldon Railroad until his death. He was founder of the North Carolina Railroad and director of the Bank of Cape Fear. The Dickinson House was torn down in 1902 to make way for the Murchison National Bank, also known as the Acme Building.

James Dawson House

The James Dawson House was located on the northwest corner of Front and Chestnut streets. James Dawson (1816-1882) was an Irish-born merchant, cotton broker and banker who settled in Wilmington permanently in the late 1840s. The house was sold to the Cape Fear Club in 1888. Organized in 1852, the club is reputed to be the oldest gentlemen's club in the South in continuous existence. The club retained ownership of the building until 1913 when it was torn down to make way for the Murchison Building.

The James Dawson House (Cape Fear Club) in the 1890s.

Mrs. Davis' Boarding House

The handsome Greek Revival-style Davis House was located on North Front Street near Princess Street. It was the townhouse of Junius Davis (1815-1862) and his wife, Ann Swann Davis (1827-1876).

During the Civil War the family went to live in on their plantation in Brunswick County. It was there that Mr. Davis died in 1862. After the war, Mrs. Davis briefly ran a boarding house in their town residence. The 1870 census of New Hanover County lists 26 persons living there—Mrs. Davis and her four children; 7 single men; two couples; two families of three; and four female servants (one with a three year old child). The house was razed shortly thereafter and replaced by commercial buildings.

Mrs. Davis' Boarding House as it looked in the 1870s.

The Robert H. Cowan House / Seaboard Air Line Co.

Robert H. Cowan House

The Robert H. Cowan House was located at 255 North Front Street. Cowan (1824-1872) was the president of the Wilmington Charlotte & Rutherford Railroad. His house later became the offices of the Seaboard Air Line Railroad Company. It was torn down about 1910.

John L. Holmes House

Attorney John L. Holmes (1826-1888) built his brick three-story residence in 1849 when he married Sally M. London (1829-1908). The townhouse, located at 401 Chestnut Street, faced the street and the side piazzas overlooked a garden. A handsome pierced-brick wall surrounded the property.

The John L. Holmes House as it appeared in the 1890s.

Donald MacRae's "Scottish Castle" on Market Street was a distictive landmark.

MacRae's Scottish Castle

The MacRae House, often referred to as "the castle," was built in 1853 for John Coffin Wood. James F. Post was the architect for the dwelling located at 713 Market Street. The original Wood house was constructed in the Italianate style, an architectural design for which Post was recognized. The building began to take its unusual form after Donald MacRae bought it in 1859. A reflection of his Scottish heritage, Mr. MacRae added bays on the southeast and southwest corners of the building. He covered the walls with stucco and had them painted gray. The windows were trimmed with stone. Machicolated ornamentation was added to make the structure look like a castle. The Union Army used the MacRae house as a hospital in 1865.

With design assistance from architect Henry Bacon, Hugh MacRae, son of Donald, remodeled the house again in 1902. He built a new entrance on the west side of the house and converted the Market Street porch into a conservatory. Extensive alterations were made to the interior of the house and modern conveniences added.

The MacRae "Castle" was used as a Yankee hospital.

Donald MacRae (1825-1892) was at various times an officer or director of the Navasssa Guano Company, the Wilmington Cotton Mills Company, the Wilmington Gaslight Company, the Wilmington and Weldon Railroad and the Bank of New Hanover. Hugh MacRae (1865-1951) was a mining engineer, cotton mill executive, street railway magnate, public utility organizer, banker, realtor and developer. Both father and son were passionate about Scottish culture, which was evident in their unique residence. "The Castle" was torn down in 1955.

The Drs. Thomas House

The Drs. William G. and George P. Thomas House stood on the northwest corner of Market and Fourth streets (319 Market). It was constructed in 1852 in the Greek Revival-style, but by 1872, Italianate brackets and spectacular double-story porches had been added. There were built-in blinds on the west side of the house protecting the porches from the late afternoon sun. Blinds of this type were very popular in tropical and subtropical climates. The dwelling was built for Dr. William G. Thomas (1818-1890), who practiced medicine in Wilmington from 1851 until his death. His obituary said, "During the yellow fever epidemic of 1862, he remained at his post and was untiring in his efforts to relieve those afflicted with that terrible disease until stricken down himself, when he was compelled to leave Wilmington, but as soon as his health was restored, he was again at his post of duty." The property was inherited by his son, Dr. George G. Thomas (1848-1920), chief surgeon for the Atlantic Coast Line Railroad. The house was demolished in 1955.

The Drs. Thomas House at Market and Fourth streets during the 1870s.

The William H. Sprunt House was constructed in 1900.

Bellamy and Sprunt Houses

Wilmington was treated to two exciting structures in 1900 when John D. Bellamy, Jr., and William H. Sprunt built their eclectic and ornate residences. Both houses exuded Queen Ann-style architectural elements. The buildings had irregular plans, tall hip roofs with projecting gables and dormers, bay windows and towers. The houses looked as if their owners were determined to leave no exterior space flat or undecorated. Duryea & Potter of New York did interior decoration of both dwellings. The *Wilmington Morning Star*, 12 November 1900, reported, "the foreman of Duryea & Potter, who had charge of the interior decorations of Hon. John D. Bellamy's residence, has returned from New York to do the interior decoration in the new residence of Mr. William H. Sprunt."

The William H. Sprunt House was located at 223 North Third Street, on the northwest corner of Third and Grace. When it was constructed it had all the modern conveniences, including an indoor kitchen and two bathrooms. A basement housed the hot water furnace and coal storage room. The house was built for William H. Sprunt (1857-1939), president of Alexander Sprunt and Sons, cotton exporters. A philanthropist, Mr. Sprunt, donated a building to house the African-American ward of James Walker Memorial Hospital and served on the hospital board of managers for thirty-eight years. He donated the Sunday school building to St. Andrews Presbyterian Church and served as Sunday school superintendent for twenty-five years. Mr. Sprunt chose to build his grand house on the north side of town, near his work in the cotton business, his civic duty at the hospital and his beloved church. When the house was razed, in 1962, it was a victim of time and place. The suburbs were growing and it was less fashionable to live on the declining north side of downtown.

The John D. Bellamy, Jr., House, located on the southeast corner of Sixth and Market streets, was actually remodeled from an earlier three-story Italianate structure that stood on the site. The only visible Italianate elements from the former house were the arched hooded window treatments on the northwest and west elevations. Charles McMillen of Wilmington was the architect for the renovations. The interior was as eclectic as the exterior. Oak, cherry and mahogany were used in elaborate woodworking schemes, including

John D. Bellamy's house, photographed around 1901 (above). The house, with its distinctive "German helmet," burned down in 1972 (below).

paneling, wainscoting and ceiling beams. The vestibule and conservatory were floored with mosaic tiles. Walls and ceilings were covered with canvas and then either painted with floral designs or covered with paneled silk or tapestries. The fireplaces had onyx facings. John D. Bellamy, Jr. (1854-1942), attorney, capitalist, manufacturer and congressman, grew up in the Bellamy Mansion across the street. His remarkable house survived until 1972 when it burned. The *Wilmington Morning Star*, 24 August 1972, reported, "The German helmet is gone now. It was among the first sections of the house to fall. The 'spike' atop the 'helmet' toppled down into the body of the building."

Springer House

The William E. Springer House, located at 214 North Second Street, was constructed about 1886. It was built in the Second Empire style, which was derived from the grand architecture of the French Second Empire of Napoleon III. The Springer house featured heavy ornamentation and had a high mansard roof with dormer windows.

Originally, houses on North Second Street had high retaining walls and steps leading up to them from the sidewalk. The configuration was similar to what can be seen today in the residential section of South Second Street. The building was the residence of William E. Springer (1848-1926), a successful businessman who sold hardware and agricultural implements. He served on the city board of aldermen and was mayor from 1903 to 1905. Although the "French" style of architecture was in vogue when Mr. Springer built his house, his neighbor, Emma Woodward MacMillan, called it a Victorian monstrosity. In 1966, she wrote, "This large three-story house was garnished with fancy colored slate, weather vanes on the four corners of the wrought iron which ran around the roof, and with every fancy device known to architects of the day of gaudy display." By 1916, the house was probably considered old fashioned because it was constantly advertised for rent or for sale. The building was demolished in the early 1950s and the site turned into a parking lot.

The William E. Springer House in the 1930s.

Vollers House

The Elizabeth Hashagen Vollers House was located at 719 Market Street. Built in 1904, the imposing Neoclassical Revival-style house was designed by Henry E. Bonitz for the wealthy widow of Luhr Vollers, a German-born businessman. Sadly, Mrs. Vollers died only three years after its construction. Their only child, Katherine E. Vollers, who resided there until her death in 1964, inherited the house. A late 1960s fire damaged the house significantly. It was torn down to make way for the Employment Security Commission building.

The Vollers House in 1908.

Part Three

Community Spaces

Wilmington's Post Office on Front Street in 1906.

U.S. Post Office
Built 1888-1891

Early post offices were housed in hotels and stores. Postmasters were paid according to the amount of mail they processed. In Wilmington, the bulk of their income came from newspapers, which were received universally through the U.S. Mail during the ante-bellum period. When the 1844 U.S. Custom house was built the post office occupied rooms in the federal facility. As early as 1868, citizens began petitioning the U.S. government for a post office building. Their request was answered in 1874 when a brick two-story building was erected on the southwest corner of Second and Chestnut streets. It contained a federal courtroom on the second floor. The lobby had 750 boxes and two general delivery windows, one for men and one for women. Eleven years later the city had outgrown the structure and lobbying began for a new building. The 1874 post office building was razed in 1891.

    The wish for a new facility was granted in 1887 when Congress appropriated $150,000 for a larger and improved post office. The southwest corner of Front and Chestnut streets was chosen as the site for a grand new building. The lot ran from Front to Second streets and was 165 feet wide. Two houses were removed to make way for the project and the cornerstone was laid in June, 1888. The architect was W.A. Feret, supervising architect of the U.S. Department of Treasury. *Harper's Weekly* (May 1888) called the architecture Italian Romanesque. The massive brownstone building with impressive Romanesque arches represented progress and growth in the Port City. The building contained the post office, weather bureau, federal courtrooms and offices for other federal agencies.

    The late Robert M. Fales lamented that the stone post office was torn down to provide employment for those suffering from the Great Depression. The building, which was only 45 years old, was torn down in 1936.

The act pitted preservationists against the Wilmington Central Labor Union and a few local politicians who agreed with them. There was an attempt by some city officials to save the building and convert it into a public library or other worthy civic building. The final decision favored demolition and Wilmington lost a grand and architecturally significant public building.

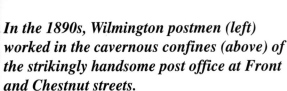

In the 1890s, Wilmington postmen (left) worked in the cavernous confines (above) of the strikingly handsome post office at Front and Chestnut streets.

Post Office Park & Woodrow Wilson Huts

The post office property was big enough to accommodate a city park behind the building. The park was laid out in quadrants with a fountain in the center. It was probably Wilmington's first public fountain, a precursor to the ones in front of the U.S. Custom House (1919) on the waterfront and the Kenan Fountain (1921) at Fifth and Market streets. The park became a gathering place for local events, a community space where all citizens of Wilmington, without deference to race or creed, could gather on a regular basis.

After World War I, the Woodrow Wilson Hut was built on the site of the fountain. It was open to soldiers and sailors stationed in the area as well as to veterans. The steamer *Wilmington* was chartered to bring soldiers stationed at Fort

Post Office Park around 1915.

33c

The 1940s Woodrow Wilson Hut (above) replaced an earlier one that dated from the end of World War I. The picture below shows that first building around 1930.

33b

Caswell to the dedication ceremony, which took place in January 1919. The Craftsman-style building had a large engaged porch that was perfect for rocking chairs. The meeting place was named for President Woodrow Wilson. His father, the Rev. Joseph R. Wilson, was minister of First Presbyterian Church from 1874 to 1885. The clubhouse provided a place for servicemen and veterans to meet, relax, have dinners and hold dances. The building was significantly damaged by fire in 1934, when it was the headquarters of American Legion Post No. 10. The structure was torn down shortly thereafter.

In 1941, a second Woodrow Wilson Hut was constructed behind City Hall at the northwest corner of Fourth and Princess streets. A city-county funded project, it was a popular place for World War II servicemen stationed in the area. The June 4, 1941 *Morning Star* reported that, "All day Sunday, soldiers from Camp Davis were making their first visits to the hut. Some were writing letters home, others merely relaxed and rested. A large number of soldiers enjoyed themselves listening to the radio or reading magazines and newspapers." Local girls attended the nightly dances. An interior room was converted into the "Cinderella Closet" that contained gowns, bags and hundreds of pairs of evening shoes. The original idea for the closet was to supply formal clothing to mothers, wives and sweethearts of soldiers who came to town without the proper attire. Instead it became the craze with local girls who didn't want to be seen wearing the same dress twice. Claude Howell drew the sketch of the second Woodrow Wilson Hut. In 1945, the building was remodeled as offices for the Chamber of Commerce. It was torn down in 1970.

1844 U.S. Custom House
& Alton Lennon Federal Building

As early as 1819, there was a customhouse on the east side of Water Street between Market and Princess streets. After the building burned in the devastating 1843 fire, it was replaced by a handsome three-story, pedimented, Greek Revival-style structure. The architect was John Norris of New York. After a few years, Norris left Wilmington and moved to Savannah, Georgia, where he designed many important buildings, including a U.S. Custom House that still stands.

When Wilmington's Custom House was completed in 1844, it faced a river crowded with vessels. The location was central to port activities. Regional customs were administered on this site for over 150 years. At one time or another, every type, shape or size of vessel imaginable docked at the government wharf in front of the Custom House. Besides customs officials, the 1844 Custom House contained other federal government offices and courtrooms. The U.S. post office was located there from 1844 to 1874.

By the turn of the twentieth century, the port of Wilmington had outgrown the 1844 building. In 1915, all buildings on Water Street between Market and Princess were razed in order to build a larger customhouse. James A. Wetmore, supervising architect of the Treasury, designed the Beaux Arts classical building that was constructed from 1916 to 1919. The wings of the three-story building retain the John Norris temple-form design of the 1844 custom house. In 1976, the building was named for Alton Asa Lennon (1906-1986), US senator (1953 and 1954) and member of the US House of Representatives (1957 to 1973).

In 1965, the U.S. Customs Appraisers moved to a building at the North Carolina State Port Authority. Although the downtown building continues to house federal offices and courtrooms, the exciting hubbub surrounding the old customhouses is a thing of the past. Gone are the days when contraband (illegal whiskey and narcotics) or unusual cargo (exotic plants and animals) would produce crowds of spectators at a moment's notice.

The 1844 Custom House (above) that stood on Water Street until it was replaced by the Alton Lennon Federal Building (below) in 1919.

The federal building was named for U.S. Congressman and Senator Alton A. Lennon in 1976.

Front Street's City Market (left) as it looked in 1910. The Market House (below) stood in the middle of Market Street at the intersection of Front Street from 1848 to 1881.

Market Houses

Wilmington's eighteenth century Market House was located in the middle of Market Street. The Town Commissioners added a story and belfry to it in 1839. A new Market House was constructed in 1848. It was located at the intersection of Front and Market streets and ran 187 feet towards the river. Built by Benjamin Gardner, the building had thirty-eight cast-iron columns and an iron roof. A tower contained a 565-pound bell. It rang at nine a.m. (open for business), at one p.m. (lunch time), and at seven p.m. (closing time). The nine o'clock curfew bell summoned all slaves to be off the streets. Stalls were rented to fruit, vegetable, seafood and meat vendors.

Most residents purchased their meat every day. During one month in 1868, the number of beef sold was 320; hog amounted to 272 and sheep, 187. Stall rent provided considerable funds for city coffers and the town commissioners passed continuous ordinances regarding the use of the building. In 1869, a force pump with a hose attached was installed to wash the brick floors. Six large lamps, illuminated by gaslight, were installed in 1878. On January 27, 1881, the building was torn down. The *Wilmington Star* lamented, "Well, another landmark is gone, and it will be missed the more from the fact it occupied so conspicuous a position."

With no room to expand and community disgust with open-air vending, a grand new Market House was constructed in 1880. It was built by the Wilmington Market Company, who rented it to the city as a public market. Located on the west side of the 100 block of South Front Street (120 S. Front St.), the building extended from Front Street to Water Street. It was 70 feet wide and 205 feet deep. Designed by J.A Vaughan, it faced Front Street and had a tower 15 feet square and 84 feet high to the base of the weathervane. The building had a belfry on the northeast corner that contained a bell and a reservoir (seven feet of water) from which the market received water for cleaning. A skylight and ventilator stretched most of the length of the building. There were three storefronts on the Front

The City Market after renovations in the 1930s.

Street side. The Market Hall contained two main avenues, four feet wide. There were sixteen side stalls and center stalls. The floor was brick and the building lighted by gaslights. A fish and oyster building was separate, located on the west side of Water Street, to keep the seafood smell out of the main building. Choice stalls were auctioned to the highest bidders. Stall prices ranged from $10 to $21 per month. In 1882, the city purchased the Market House.

In 1930, the towers were torn off and the facade was redesigned in the Mission Revival-style of architecture. The market continued to operate into the 1950s. The city council sold it in 1960 and the building became a warehouse. Deserted for over a decade, the 16,000-square-foot building was opened as the Wilmington City Market on March 20, 1993.

Wilmington Railroads

Wilmington's 125 year association with the railroad began in 1834-35 when the Wilmington and Raleigh Rail Road was chartered. The first tracts were laid from Wilmington to Weldon, North Carolina, and the inaugural run occurred in 1840. The name of the company was changed to Wilmington and Weldon Railroad in 1855. Both Wilmington and the railroad grew exponentially as other railroad companies opened offices in Wilmington. By 1900, many lines were consolidated into the Atlantic Coast Line Railroad (ACL) and the Port City became the headquarters of a major southeastern railroad. The railroad buildings were located around Front and Red Cross streets. The tracks and yards were north of Red Cross. The complex included office buildings, warehouses, a roundhouse, a passenger terminal, freight terminals and shops where railway cars were repaired and constructed. The various yards were well supplied

The Atlantic Coast Line Railroad General Offices, circa 1905.

Union Station, circa 1915.

with sheds and other utility buildings. Two buildings of note were the General Office Building and Union Station.

Beginning in 1889, the Wilmington and Weldon Railroad constructed an impressive three-story brick office building on the west side of Front Street between Walnut and Red Cross streets. By 1900 two more sections were added. The building had a central bell tower and beautiful arched doors and windows. After the

Wilmington's Atlantic Coast Line Railroad complex in the 1950s.

ACL left Wilmington, urban renewal took its toll on the abandoned building. It was demolished in 1962. The site became part of the campus of Cape Fear Technical College, now Cape Fear Community College.

Union Station, the most memorable of the railroad buildings, was built in 1913. The name was derived, like all other Union Stations in the country, from the union of more than one railroad. Joseph F. Leitner of Wilmington designed the Neoclassical Revival-style building. The fluted pilasters with Ionic capitals that adorned the facade were repeated in the Ionic column that supported the enclosed concourse that crossed North Front Street. The multi-faced clock atop the column became a city landmark. The building was abandoned after the ACL left Wilmington. During the 1960s there were attempts to find a use for the former station. Finally, an architect hired by the city reported that the building was not very old, was of little architectural significance and since they could find no tenants, it should be torn down. Union Station was demolished in 1970.

The demolition of Union Station in 1970.

Wilmington was a railroad town on December 10, 1955 (Black Thursday), when the Atlantic Coast Line Railroad revealed plans to relocate the company headquarters to Jacksonville, Florida. By 1960, the transition was complete and over thirteen hundred employees and their families transferred from Wilmington. The company gave the vacated railroad buildings to the city. Reeling from the loss of an eight million dollar payroll, the city could find no practical use for the buildings. At the same time urban renewal became a popular source of funding for demolition of inner-city buildings and subsequently most of the railroad buildings were demolished within ten years. Eventually the tracks were removed creating a virtual wasteland north of Red Cross Street. Forty years later, plans were completed to construct a convention center and hotel on the site.

The former site of the Atlantic Coast Line Railroad's general offices, that were replaced by Cape Fear Technical Institute.

Bluethenthal Field

Wilmington Airport in the 1920s.

As early as 1911, aviation pioneers held exhibitions in Wilmington. On March 12, 1911, the *Morning Star* reported, "Driving his machine against a fierce overhead wind at the rate of about a mile a minute, at an altitude estimated at 4,000 feet, Lincoln Beachy yesterday between 4 and 5 o'clock, made the most sensational and spectacular flight of the big meet here, when he journeyed in his aero plane from the fair grounds in the city and after hovering for a brief moment over the Cape Fear River, circled the town."

Flying became routine after World War I, which had given large numbers of men the opportunity to learn how to fly. In the early 1920s, when passenger service became more common, Wilmington officials were anxious to provide a landing field for the lucrative north-south route from New York to Miami. They constructed a municipal airfield several miles from the city near Gordon Road. In 1928, it was dedicated and named Bluethenthal Memorial Air Field, in honor of the first Wilmingtonian to lose his life in the war, aviator Arthur Bluethenthal.

The original aircraft hanger in the 1930s.

The 1928 hanger just before its demolition.

The first hangar was constructed in 1929. The contractor was U. A. Underwood and the cost was $4,200. The bowstring truss hangar measured 60 feet by 80 feet. The hangar survived until 1987. One year before, a survey of historic structures in New Hanover County stated that "the small hangar is especially important as an example of engineering technology of its period and for its direct relation to the history of aviation in the region." The surveyors suggested that the county nominate the hangar to the National Register of Historic Places. About the same time, local preservationists discovered that it was the oldest surviving aviation building in the state and one of the oldest in the nation. Several historical aviation organizations were interested dismantling the structure and moving it to a museum setting. Unfortunately, without any warning, the structure was demolished and the site cleared of salvage.

Pennington Flying Service, circa 1950.

In 1942, the airport was taken over by the U.S. Army Air Corps. It was returned to the county in 1945 and commercial flights resumed. Piedmont Airlines' first flight- Flight 41- took off from the airport on February 20, 1948. The DC-3 airliner stopped at Pinehurst, Charlotte, Asheville, Johnson City, Tennessee, and Lexington, Kentucky, before landing in Cincinnati, Ohio, four and one half hours later. The familiar sight of a Piedmont plane ended when USAir acquired the North Carolina-based company in the late 1980s. A new terminal that was dedicated on September 15, 1990, replaced the Bluethenthal Airport Terminal Building. The 1952 brick control tower and a World War II-vintage hangar with iron roof trusses and concrete buttresses survive. In 2003, a group of flight enthusiasts formed a committee to explore the possibility of creating an aviation museum at the airport, to preserve the buildings that are left and record the area's rich aviation history. They became the Wilmington Aviation Foundation, which is devoted to making the North Carolina Museum of Aviation a success at old Bluethenthal Field.

For years Piedmont Airlines was the main carrier at Wilmington's airport (left),which by the 1970s had grown much larger than its humble roots (below).

Seaman's Bethel

During the early decades of the nineteenth century, seamen were reluctant to sail into Wilmington because of poor medical facilities. In 1835, humane citizens subscribed $1,894 for the relief of suffering sailors and formed the Wilmington Marine Hospital Association. A facility for seamen called the Marine Hotel was built at the southwest corner of Front and Dock streets. In 1853, the recently organized Seaman's Friend Society purchased it. A charitable group, the Society was founded and funded by local businessmen. It provided refuge, care and religion to large numbers of sailors from all over the world. During the Civil War, the Seaman's Home (later referred to as the Seaman's Bethel) became Confederate General Hospital No. 4. On October 1, 1864, the body of Confederate spy Rose O'Neale Greenhow, who drowned near Ft. Fisher, laid in state at the Seaman's Home Chapel for most of the day before her burial. After the fall of Wilmington, Federal troops

Seaman's Bethel in 1900. An earlier building was a Confederate military hospital during the Civil War.

occupied the building. They damaged it severely and stole the furniture, doors, windows and even the mosquito netting.

The pre-war building was replaced in 1873 by a four-story brick structure that was covered with stucco. It measured 61 feet square and had a handsome mansard roof. The bottom floor was rented to businesses and the top three floors had rooms for seamen. It was designed and built by James F. Post. In 1914, the building suffered extensive fire damages and the mansard roof was removed. In 1958, the building was razed after another bad fire. The lot remained empty until the 1990s, when the Reel Cafe was constructed. During excavation for the building many relics of the former Seaman's Bethel were unearthed.

The Seaman's Bethel in the 1930s.

Marine Hospital

The Marine Hospital was located at the southwest corner of Eighth and Nun streets. The architect was Ammi B. Young and the builder, James Walker. The two-story brick building was covered with stucco and had an octagonal cupola. The wings had double piazzas that extended around the sides of the structure. An interior circular iron staircase rose from the basement to the cupola. The building was constructed about 1857 when the U.S. Treasury Department purchased the land for the project. During the Civil War, it became General Hospital No. 5 and had a Confederate encampment in the yard. Physicians liked the location of the hospital because it was so isolated. Convalescents were not as easily distracted as they would have been in the boisterous downtown and there was ample room on the fifty acre site for a garden. During World War II, the site was used to house German POWS. The building was torn down in 1950.

The isolated Marine Hospital around 1900 (top right), and as it looked just after World War II (bottom right).

40a

WILMINGTON CITY HOSPITAL.

Founded in 1881, Conjointly by the City of Wilmington and New Hanover County.

WM. W. LANE, A. M., M. D., SUPERINTENDENT,
SURGEON IN CHARGE.

WL DE ROSSET JR.
PHOTO ENG
WILMINGTON,
NC

City Hospital as it looked in 1891, a decade after it opened.

City Hospital

Founded in 1881, the area's first publicly funded hospital was City Hospital. The facility was housed in a remodeled structure already on the property. Located at Tenth and Red Cross streets, it was accessible by horse or carriage, or from Fourth Street, by a wooden sidewalk. A whites-only establishment, it had no interior facilities for African-American patients until 1888, when a one-story detached ward was added. The hospital was torn down in 1890 to make room for James Walker Memorial Hospital.

James Walker Memorial Hospital

Construction of the four-story red brick James Walker Memorial Hospital began in 1900. Located on two city blocks between Tenth and Eleventh streets and Grace and Red Cross streets, the fifty-bed facility with modern equipment was a great source of civic pride. The architect, Kenneth M. Murchison of New York, had family ties in Wilmington. The hospital was a gift from James Walker (1828-1901), a Scottish-

James Walker Memorial Hospital in 1907.

born immigrant who came to the United States in
the 1840s. A builder, he worked on the U.S.
Capitol Building and the Smithsonian Institution
in Washington, D.C. before he moved to
Wilmington in 1857 to construct the Marine
Hospital. He remained in Wilmington until his
death in 1901. Sadly, he died before the hospital
was completed.

Local philanthropists donated other
buildings. In 1904, William H. Sprunt built an
annex that housed a ward for African-American
patients and a dormitory for nurses. James and
Luola Murchison Sprunt endowed the Marian
Sprunt Annex in 1904. Built in memory of their
daughter, who died of scarlet fever, the annex
contained a thirty-three-bed maternity and
children's ward. The Samuel Bear Building was
given in 1909. The Nurses' Quarters were
financed by donations in memory of the Rev.
A.D. McClure, a beloved Presbyterian minister
who died in 1920. Only one building remains
from the hospital complex that filled most of
three city blocks. The buildings were demolished
after New Hanover Memorial Hospital opened in
1967.

The hospital in the 1950s (below), and 1960s (above).

*Community Hospital
catered to Wilmington's
African-American
community during the
days of segregation. The
first hospital building
was housed in the former
Niestlie's Drug Store.*

Community Hospital

I n 1998, local historian, Bill Reaves wrote, "Good medical facilities, crucial to the well-being of society, have always been difficult to obtain. The enormous costs involved make the task extra-daunting, especially in minority communities. The story of how Wilmington's African-American community obtained decent medical facilities is truly a story of their 'strength through struggle'."

Although City Hospital and James Walker Memorial Hospital maintained wards for African-Americans, these facilities were insufficient. Also, during the era of segregation, African-American physicians and surgeons were unable to hold positions of authority. Unlike other cities in the state, Wilmington did not have an African-American infirmary. In 1920, Dr. Foster F. Burnett (1894-1945) spearheaded an effort to rectify the situation. The organizers of what became Community Hospital raised $25,000 to remodel and equip a building at 417 North Seventh Street. It was the former drugstore and residence of William Niestlie. Renovation

Community Hospital's second home in 1965.

plans were prepared by W.J. Wilkins & Company, architects, and the contractor was Al Harris. The newspaper reported that over a thousand people attended the dedication ceremony of Community Hospital, which was held on February 1, 1921. Black and white physicians, the mayor and many dignitaries from across the state were present.

At the end of the first year of business, 368 persons had been admitted to the hospital and 1,000 seen in the clinics. For the next eighteen years this small hospital ran at full to overflowing capacity. There were many times when patients were assigned to pallets on the floor or very sick patients had to be sent home before they were ready. However, the institution survived through constant fund raising activities in the African-American community. Help was also received from a biracial group of physicians, who donated their services.

Relief came in 1938 when the Works Progress Administration (WPA) announced that they would provide forty-five percent of the funding for a new building. The city and county pledged the rest. Wilmington architect James B. Lynch designed the new hospital at 511 South Eleventh Street. The cornerstone, laid on June 29, 1939, was transferred from the old building to the new one, symbolizing the continuity and history of the hospital. Governor Clyde R. Hoey gave the dedication address one month later. A two-story home for nurses was built in 1940. During World War II an increase in defense workers resulted in the building of an annex. Community Hospital was a first-class accredited institution with a reputation for an excellent nursing school. In 1967, it was closed when the integrated New Hanover Memorial Hospital opened its doors.

Dr. Charles Harper's privately owned hospital at the corner of Front and Castle streets in 1912.

Harper's Sanitarium

During the first half of the twentieth century, small privately owned hospitals were popular. Harper's Sanitarium, located on northeast corner of Front and Castle streets, was built in 1910 in the Mission Revival-style of architecture. Dr. Charles T. Harper accepted patients who suffered from any kind of malady that was non-contagious.

Southside Drugs occupied the Harper building in the 1950s (left). The same building after demolition in 1970 (above).

In 1912, Dr. Harper added a third story to the building that contained a kitchen, dining room, an operating room and more patient rooms. The building accommodated forty patients and Dr. Harper employed five nurses. The architect who designed the third-story addition and interior improvements was Joseph F. Leitner. The mansard roof, which had been out of vogue for a generation, was made entirely out of wood. Dr. Harper died in 1915 and the building was never used as a hospital again. From 1910 to 1963, Southside Drug Company occupied the ground floor of the building. Privately owned neighborhood pharmacies were common until the last decades of the twentieth century when they were almost universally replaced by drugstore chains. The building was demolished in 1970.

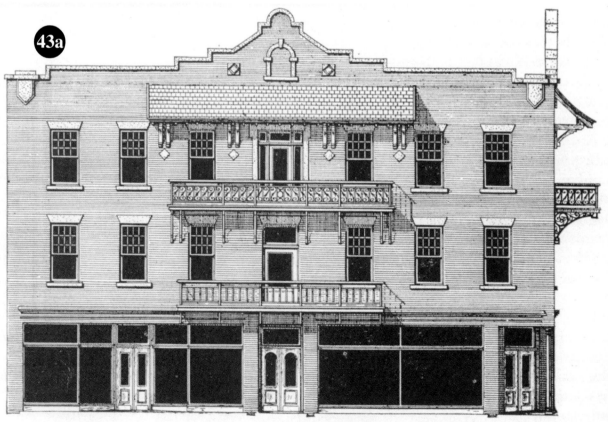

Harper's Sanitorium in 1910.

Nurses from Babies Hospital with their young charges pose on the front lawn in 1935.

Babies Hospital

Babies Hospital opened its doors to sick infants and children in 1920. The idea of a pediatric hospital belonged to Dr. James Buren Sidbury (1886-1967) who received his medical degree from Columbia University and did postgraduate work in pediatric hospitals in New York City. He moved to Wilmington in 1915. The first Babies Hospital was a converted wood-frame beach cottage overlooking Wrightsville Sound. Many of the furnishings, equipment and supplies were donated. Double story porches were screened to prevent insects from attacking the children while they breathed fresh ocean air. The facility had 22 beds and served 83 patients its first summer season.

A novel idea, Dr. Sidbury encouraged mothers to stay in the hospital where they could comfort their children and learn from the staff how to properly take care of them. From the beginning, the hospital accepted

A color view of Babies Hospital in the 1930s.

The demolition of Babies Hospital in January 2004.

charity patients. Endowing a charity bed for the summer cost $200. Annexes were added to the building in 1921 and 1924. On May 29, 1927, the building caught fire. No one was injured but the structure was a total loss.

On June 15, 1928, a two-story fireproof hospital opened across the road from the original building. Charles Hartman of Greensboro designed the Mediterranean-style building. On each end of the handsome brick building were two-story screened porches where the patients could rest and breathe healthy sea air. In 1939, the hospital became year-round. In 1955, a gift from Dr. Sidbury and his wife provided the funding for a nurses' home on the property. Jessie Kenan Wise endowed a third story in 1956. Dr. Sidbury was the director of the facility from 1920 until his death in 1967. Ironically, he died the same year that the hospital experienced its greatest usage.

Changing trends in pediatrics care and the increased centralization of health care facilities in New Hanover County were cited as reasons for terminating Babies Hospital. In 1978, the institution closed at the end of the summer. During the ensuing years the building was sold and converted into office space. The North Carolina Department of Health and Natural Resources rented space there from 1980 to 1991. In 1996, rumors of demolition caused preservationists to begin a long battle with developers over the fate of the building. Despite the efforts of countless citizens the historically significant building was razed on Friday, January 23, 2004.

Wilmington's YMCA in 1920.

YMCA

A 1902 Chamber of Commerce publication boasted, "The Young Men's Christian Association has a handsome building along the line of the principal thoroughfare of the city, where visitors to Wilmington are always welcome." Located on the northwest corner of Front and Grace streets, the "Y" was only a few blocks away from the railroad passenger terminal. Built in 1891, it provided rooms for visitors and had an auditorium and swimming pool for members. The three-story brick building was massive. The entrance to the "Y" faced Front Street. Next-door were two first floor storefronts. The building extended down the slope of Chestnut Street toward the river and had a full basement. The structure was used as a YMCA for twenty-two years. Afterwards, it housed several hotels. The building was razed in 1970 during urban renewal.

In 1913, the YMCA moved into a new building on the north side of Market Street, between Third and Fourth streets. It was five stories tall and the entire

45a

The Young Men's Christian Association was located at Front and Grace streets in 1907.

building was devoted to "Y" activities. It had a swimming pool, meeting rooms and an auditorium. The upper floor rooms were rented by the day, week or month. A similar building is still standing in Columbia, South Carolina. In 1970, the "Y" moved to a modern one-story building at 2710 Market Street. The old building was demolished shortly thereafter.

Ruth Hall

Located at 401 South Seventh Street, Ruth Hall was the headquarters of the Wilmington Grand Order of the Odd Fellows. When the building was dedicated in 1888, the *Morning Star* reported, "This building is quite a handsome brick structure, three stories in height, and is of the most improved order of architecture. The third story is used as a hall for the fraternity exclusively, and the floors below are a commodious concert hall and lecture room fitted in modern style with an elevated stage, galleries, etc." For sixty years it was a cultural center for Wilmington's African-American community. Dances, concerts, lectures and conventions, as well as patriotic and fraternal meetings were held there. In the 1930s, Ruth Hall's regular dances featured nationally renowned bands. Snookums Russell, Harley Toots and Bill Davidson and his Ambassadors Orchestra were among the many dance bands that played at Ruth Hall. Neighborhood children remember sitting outside and listening to the lively music until late in the evening. Ruth Hall was torn down in the 1940s.

46a

Ruth Hall in 1905.

The Boys Brigade Armory in 1908.

Boys Brigade Armory

The Boys Brigade Armory, located on the southeast corner of Church and Second streets, was built in 1904. The Brigade, an organization for underprivileged boys, was organized and funded by local businessmen, including its most ardent supporter, Col. Walker Taylor. The clubhouse was a gift from Mary Lily Kenan Flagler as a memorial to her brother, William Rand Kenan, a Brigade supporter and friend of Col. Taylor. The architect was Charles McMillen and the contractor was R. H. Brady. The building was located in Dry Pond, a working class neighborhood. The boys could easily walk or ride their bikes to the armory. Built out of artificial stone, the masculine design of the armory probably appealed to the imagination of the boys. It featured a bowling alley, dining room, auditorium and a gymnasium. The building eventually became apartments and was torn down circa 1962.

Williston School

The history of Williston School is a lengthy one. The institution dates back to the American Missionary Association, which funded schools for African-Americans after the Civil War. The school was named for Samuel Williston, a northern philanthropist who made large donations to the AMA educational fund. In 1873, Williston became part of the city's school system. Classes were held in a wood-frame, two-story building located on South Seventh Street between Ann and Nun streets. This school building was demolished in 1915 and a handsome new one erected at Tenth and Church streets. Renamed Williston Primary and Industrial School, the institution focused on vocational courses. The campus was large enough to support gardens where students learned modern techniques in crop cultivation. Two annexes were added to this building, but by the late 1920s it was deemed too small for the growing student body.

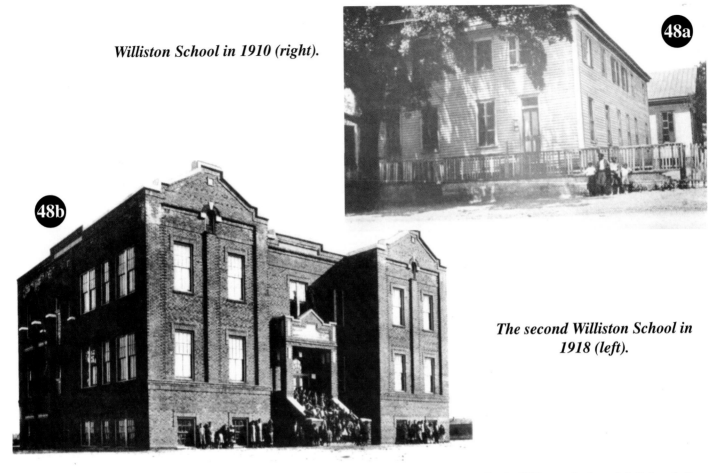

Williston School in 1910 (right).

The second Williston School in 1918 (left).

A third school building was constructed on the same site in 1931. Called Williston Industrial School, it was destroyed by fire only five years later. In 1936, it was replaced by a new building that was nearly identical to the one that burned. This building survives as Gregory Elementary School.

In 1953, a million dollar modern high school was built on the campus. Williston High School excelled in academics, music, sports and civic responsibility. In 1968, when the New Hanover County Schools were integrated, Williston High School closed. It was replaced by a junior high school that eventually became a middle school.

Williston School in 1931 (left).

Williston High School in 1966 (right).

Over the years, Williston was known as a premier educational institution for African-Americans. The school inhabited many buildings, educated many talented students and provided educational leadership in the community. It was also the center for important and enriching social events. The Williston Alumni Association, an active and vibrant group, which gives scholarships to African-American students, keeps the history and legacy of Williston alive.

Tileston School

Tileston School, located at 412 Ann Street, was built in 1871-72. The architect of the Italianate-style building was John A. Fox of Boston, Massachusetts. The school building was placed in the center of the property that covered half of a city block. The east and west elevations of the original building can still be viewed from Fifth Avenue and Fourth Street. The structure had a cupola that measured eight feet square and was eleven feet high. When the cupola windows were raised warm air funneled out and cooler air circulated through the building. The first floor contained four classrooms and the second floor had an exhibition hall and stage. The school building was a gift from New England philanthropist, Mary Tileston Hemenway. She also paid for school operations during the first twenty years.

After Mrs. Hemenway's death, the school was leased to the city. In 1901, it reopened as Wilmington High School. A Neo-Classical Revival-style front annex was added in 1915. Designed by Joseph F. Leitner, it changed the entire look of the building. The rear wing and stair hall, designed by Henry E. Bonitz, was added in 1919. Leslie N. Boney, Sr., designed the 1937 wings to the Ann Street annex.

Tileston became an elementary school when New Hanover High School opened in 1922. It remained a public school until 1986, when preservationists lost a fight to keep the state's

49a

49b

Tileston School in 1890 (above), and in 1901 (right). Tileston is now owned by St. Mary Catholic Church.

oldest school building in continuous use from closing. Janet Seapker, president of the Historic Wilmington Foundation, summed up the cause when she said, "Renovating existing buildings is much cheaper than new construction and downtown Wilmington is becoming a popular place to live. The school is near museums, the library and the river." After sitting empty for several years, the historic building was purchased by St. Mary Catholic Church.

Union "Home School" in 1890 (above), "Big Union" (below) in 1895.

Union School

Union Home School (shown above) was erected in 1856 on South Sixth Street between Nun and Church streets. The term 'Union" was given to any educational institution that was funded by both public and private funds. Wilmington's early attempt to provide public/private education was ended by the Civil War. Supported by the Soldiers Memorial Society of Boston and the American Unitarian Association, the school reopened in the winter of 1865-66 as the Union School House. The building, which came to be called Home School, was abandoned in 1891.

In 1872, Union School ("Little Union") was taken over by the public school system and relocated to a wooden building on Ann Street between Fifth and Sixth streets. By 1887, the school had 375 students. In March 1891, the building burned. By October, when the students returned from summer vacation, "Big Union" was ready for them. A grammar school, Union served the south side community from Dock to Castle streets. It was torn down in the 1920s.

Hemenway Elementary School in 1917.

Hemenway Hall

After the Civil War, the American Unitarian Association and the Soldiers' Memorial Society of Boston sent Miss Amy Morris Bradley (1823-1904) to Wilmington to open a school called the "Wilmington Mission." Miss Bradley contacted a wealthy philanthropist and friend, Mary Tileston Hemenway, to help fund the project. In 1870-71, a school was built near the corner of Fourth and Campbell streets and named Hemenway School in honor of its benefactor. In 1896, a second Hemenway School was constructed at 210 North Fifth Avenue. By 1914, the school was too small and congested. It was replaced by an attractive brick three-story Neo-Classical Revival-style school building that opened in 1915. Hemenway was an elementary school until 1962 when it became the offices of the New Hanover County Board of Education and renamed Hemenway Hall. A fire destroyed the building on May 16, 1971. The blaze also incinerated thousands of New Hanover County school records dating back to 1897. The building was a total loss and was razed. The Hemenway name, associated with schools in Wilmington for 100 years, is remembered now as Hemenway Park located at the same site.

Isaac Bear School

In 1912, Samuel Bear Jr. (1854-1916) donated $30,000 to the County Board of Education to build a school. The gift was a memorial to his brother, Isaac Bear (1852-1911). Both brothers were active in Wilmington civic affairs. Samuel Bear served on the School Committee for many years.

Located on the south side of the 1200 block of Market Street, the elementary school served the children on the eastern side of the city. The brick two-story building had six classrooms, an auditorium and playrooms. When it opened there were seven teachers and 275 pupils. The school was enlarged twice, in 1923 and in 1930. Isaac Bear School closed in 1942, when the children were assigned to the new Chestnut Street School. It became an annex for New Hanover High School, located across the street.

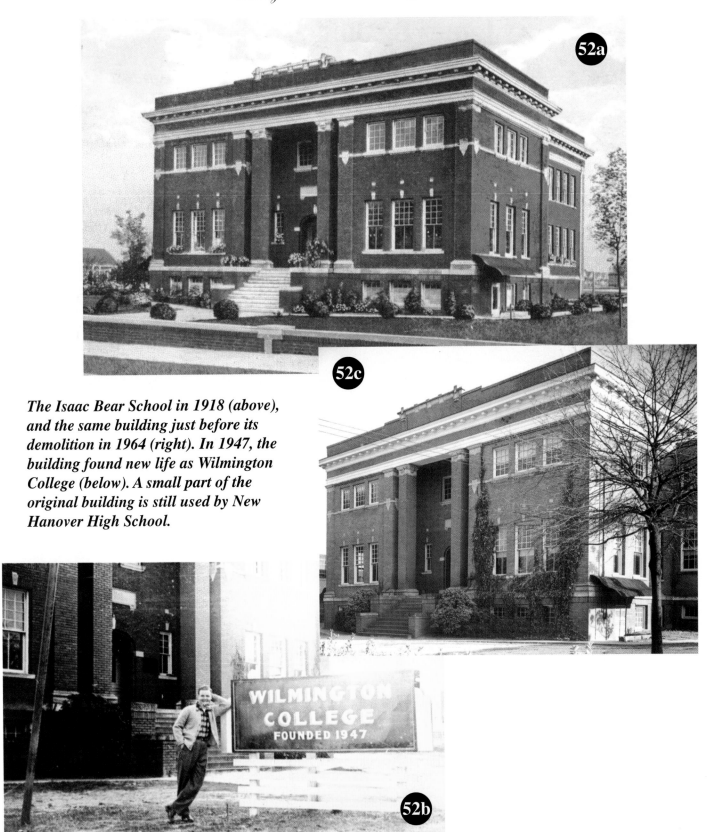

The Isaac Bear School in 1918 (above), and the same building just before its demolition in 1964 (right). In 1947, the building found new life as Wilmington College (below). A small part of the original building is still used by New Hanover High School.

Isaac Bear Hall of New Hanover High School was revived in 1947 as the location of Wilmington College, which was founded to bring post-secondary education to World War II veterans. In 1956, the college took possession of the entire building. The institution moved to Highway 132 (College Road) in 1962. It became a four-year institution in 1964 and joined the University of North Carolina system in 1969. The Isaac Bear building was torn down about 1965. A small portion remains as an annex for New Hanover High School.

James B. Dudley School

James B. Dudley School in 1950 (above).

The Neo-Classical Revival-style James B. Dudley School, located at 920 North Sixth Street, was constructed in 1914. From 1914 to 1942, it was known as Cornelius Harnett School in honor of the Revolutionary patriot. White children were educated there until it closed in 1942. It reopened in 1949 with an African-American student body. In 1952, the school was renamed for James B. Dudley, a Wilmington native and educator who became the president of North Carolina Agricultural and

The same building in disrepair in 2000.

Technical College in Greensboro. After integration, the school was used to educate children of both races. James B. Dudley School closed in 1983, but the Head Start program remained there until 1987. From that time repeated attempts to save the building failed. The monumental Ionic columns fell and were removed from the site. In 2005, the building was declared a hazard and condemned to demolition.

Wrightsboro School

Wrightsboro School dates back to a wooden two-room schoolhouse that was built on land given by Moses Horne in 1909. The New Hanover County Board of Education purchased three acres of land from Mr. Horne in 1924 and built a one-story brick building on the property. A second story was added in 1939. The building survives with several more additions.

Wrightsboro School and students around 1915.

The Academy of Incarnation in 1920.

Academy of Incarnation

The Sisters of Charity of Our Lady of Mercy were the first nuns to work in North Carolina. They made their initial appearance in 1862 when they were sent to Wilmington to nurse victims of the yellow fever epidemic. In 1869, the Vicar Apostolic of North Carolina, James Gibbons (later Cardinal), petitioned the Sisters of Mercy in Charleston, South Carolina to send a small group of nuns to Wilmington permanently. The sisters arrived in Wilmington on September 21, 1869. Shortly thereafter, they opened the first Catholic school in the state. A convent and school was established in the Benjamin Beery house (202 Nun Street) and the first commencement of the Academy of Sisters of Mercy occurred there in 1870.

The school name changed to the Academy of Incarnation (female academy) when the sisters moved to the former Henry Peden house located on the east side of Fourth Street between Orange and Ann streets. They lived and taught school in the handsome Greek Revival-style dwelling (circa 1845) that was surrounded by a beautiful pierced-brick wall. In 1873, an Italianate-style school building was constructed south of the house. In 1954, the buildings were replaced by a modern brick building that continues at the turn of the twenty-first century as St. Mary Parochial School.

St. James Church

The act of legislature (1739-40) that incorporated the town of Wilmington called for the erection of an Anglican church. In 1751, the legislature authorized a tax to raise money to supplement personal gifts already made to build a church. Construction of St. James Church began in 1751, but the building was not completed until the

An artist's conception of the 1770 St. James Church.

early 1770s. Prior to construction, church services were held in the courthouse. The brick Georgian style church building was consecrated in 1770. The eighteenth century building and burying ground were located on the south side of Market Street between Third and Fourth streets. Services were held there until March 25, 1839, when the building was demolished prior to construction of the present church building.

St. Philips Church, built at Colonial Brunswick Town, as it looked in 1905.

St. Philips Church

The ruin of St. Philips Church, in Brunswick Town, is reminiscent of the colony's eighteenth century brick church buildings. St. Philips was constructed from 1754 to 1758. The British burned it in 1776 and it was never rebuilt. The beautiful Georgian-style church featured Flemish bond brickwork and arched windows. Grand in scale, the church was 52 feet wide and 76 feet long. The walls of the ruin, which no longer support a roof, are 22 feet high.

St. Philips Church characterizes Brunswick Town's importance as a colonial port and seat of government. Abandoned by 1830, Brunswick Town became part of Orton Plantation in 1842. During the Civil War (1862) the site became Fort Anderson, a fort built to protect Wilmington. The church ruin survived a heavy bombardment by the U.S. Navy near the end of the war. The Sprunt family, owners of Orton, gave the property to the state of North Carolina in 1952 to be preserved as a state historic site. Over the years, the ruin has been a gathering place for local residents to worship on special occasions and to commemorate their heritage.

St. John's Episcopal Church

St. James Parish established St. John's Episcopal Church in 1851. The cornerstone was laid in 1853 and the new church was dedicated in 1855. Designed by Willis and Dudley of New York, the Gothic Revival-style building was located on the northeast corner of Third and Red Cross streets. St. John's was as large as its parent church and most of its members lived on the north side of town. St. John's Parish was formed in 1860. The first rector, the Rev. J. A. Wainwright, M.D., was ordained at St. John's the same year.

St. John's Church in 1857.

When North Carolina seceded in 1861, Wainwright and his wife, whose sympathies were with the Union, left town in a closed carriage under cover of night. It was a difficult time for the fledgling congregation and their membership dwindled. St. John's was not consecrated until 1867. The church rebounded during the tenure (1870-1880) of the Rev. George Patterson, D.D. and continued to grow under the direction of the Rev. James Carmichael, S.T.D (1883-1907).

The church thrived in downtown Wilmington until after World War II, when residents began moving to the suburbs. In the early 1950s, the congregation made the difficult decision to move to the Forest Hills subdivision. Robert McClure wrote in a 2003 history of the church that: "The need was apparent. The buildings were old and the church, which once stood in a prosperous residential neighborhood, was now surrounded by garages, grocery stores, railroad yards and dilapidated houses. Without air conditioning, closing the windows during the summer services was not an option." The church building was torn down after the congregation moved out in the spring of 1954.

Front Street Methodist Church

Front Street Methodist Church, organized as an outgrowth of eighteenth century circuit work, was the second oldest church in Wilmington. A Methodist meeting house existed in Wilmington as early as 1798. A Methodist church, built in 1816, was destroyed in the terrible fire of 1843 that burned so hot it melted the railroad tracks. The cornerstone was laid for a new edifice on April 2, 1844. The congregation

Front Street Methodist Church as it looked in the 1880s.

constructed a very substantial brick building in the Greek Revival-style. It had a beautiful Greek temple facade and massive Doric columns. Located at 400 North Front Street, the church was named Front Street Methodist Church, South.

The city suffered another disastrous fire in 1886. The blaze spread from a steamboat on to a combustible wharf near the foot of Walnut Street. Front Street Methodist Church was among the many buildings that were destroyed. The congregation decided not to rebuild on the same site and they removed their old burial ground to Oakdale Cemetery.

Grace Methodist Church

After their church burned in 1886, the congregation of Front Street Methodist Church purchased land on the northeast corner of Fourth and Mulberry streets. In 1887, construction began on Grace Methodist Church, South. The new edifice was dedicated in 1890. During the interim, worship services were held at the Temple of Israel whose members had generously offered the use of their building. From 1890 to 1893, Grace Church's membership grew from 653 to 1,893. In honor of the church, the city changed the name of Mulberry Street to Grace Street in 1895. In 1916, a Sunday School Annex, designed by Burett Stephens, was constructed on the north side of the building.

On March 21, 1947, a fire started in a church storage room. Before the night was over, the roof had

collapsed and the sanctuary was destroyed. The main church building was a total loss, but the Sunday School Annex survived. Harold E. Wagoner of Philadelphia was chosen to design a new building. It opened in 1950, before the Atlantic Coast Line's decision to leave Wilmington. If the church had burned a few years later, the congregation might have chosen to abandon their downtown building and move to the suburbs. Fortunately, it survives as an historical and architectural landmark on the north side of downtown.

Grace Methodist Church in 1895. Church members met at Temple of Israel until the building was finished in 1890.

Wilmington's first A.M.E. Zion Church, St. Luke's in 1900.

St. Luke's A.M.E. Zion Church

St. Luke's was the first African Methodist Episcopal Zion church in Wilmington. The congregation grew out of Front Street Methodist Church, which in 1865 had at least 1,000 African-American members. After the Civil War, black members left the church to form their own congregations. When Bishop James Walker Hood visited Wilmington in 1865, he convinced the congregation to come with him into Zion. From these beginnings, St. Luke's has been a visible force in the spiritual, educational and cultural fabric of the city. Originally called Christian Chapel, the first building was constructed prior 1869. Located on the northeast corner of Seventh and Church streets, the chapel burned in 1878. To coincide with the construction of a new building the church was renamed St. Luke's A.M.E. Zion Church. Dedicated in 1882, the Gothic Revival-style replacement was a grand architectural addition to the city's south side. On Sunday, January 2, 1944, the 66-year-old building was destroyed by fire. Despite a World War II shortage of building supplies, a more fireproof St. Luke's was rebuilt on the same site.

First Presbyterian Church in 1910.

First Presbyterian Church

Three fires have plagued First Presbyterian Church. Dating from 1818, the first church building was located on the east side of South Front Street between Dock and Orange streets. It burned in 1819 and another church was constructed on the same site. Church Alley was named for the location of these early churches. After the second building burned in 1859, property was purchased at 121 South Third Street and Samuel Sloan of Philadelphia was engaged to design the new edifice. The elegant Gothic Revival-style church was dedicated on April 28, 1861. One of its most beloved ministers was the Rev. Joseph R. Wilson who served from 1874 to 1885. His son, Woodrow Wilson, became the 28th President of the United States. On the night of December 31, 1925, First Presbyterian Church burned for the third time. It was a total loss. A new Gothic Revival-style church, designed by Hobart Upjohn of New York, replaced the former building. First Presbyterian remained downtown during the 1950s and 1960s when many churches moved to the suburbs and it has become a significant historical and architectural landmark on the south side of downtown.

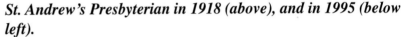

St. Andrew's Presbyterian in 1918 (above), and in 1995 (below left).

St. Andrew's Presbyterian Church

St. Andrew's Presbyterian Church, located at 420 North Fourth Street, was constructed in 1888-89. Organized in 1858 as Second Presbyterian, its parent church was First Presbyterian Church. St. Andrew's drew congregants from the growing north side of town. When the church opened it had seating for 800. A manse was built in 1908 and Sprunt Memorial Hall was added in 1910.

St. Andrew's moved out of the building in 1944, when it associated with Church of the Covenant, located at 1417 Market Street (St. Andrew's-Covenant Church). In 1962, the building was purchased by Holy Trinity Church. Their dynamic leader, the Rev. James Forbes, Jr., made it one of the leading African-American churches in the city. Later, The Rev. Forbes became pastor of the well-known Riverside Church in New York City. In the late 1980s, the church building fell victim to vandalism. Holy Trinity Church, which had moved into the Sprunt Annex, made repeated attempts to salvage the main sanctuary. In 1995, the building was condemned and the congregation moved out. Lightning hit the building, tearing a gash in the north wall. A few days later a windstorm turned the gash into a large hole in the gabled roof.

It took a group of passionate preservationists four years to save the church building that nobody wanted. The Historic Wilmington Foundation purchased the building and stabilized it. At the same time, through the efforts of the Foundation, the building was recognized as one of 300 Save America's Treasures projects. The city council used federal funding to purchase the stabilized building from the Foundation in 1999. In 2003, Dave Nathans purchased the church building and manse from the city. Renovation began in 2005 to convert the church and manse into a multi-use arts center and offices.

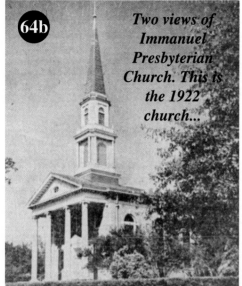

Two views of Immanuel Presbyterian Church. This is the 1922 church...

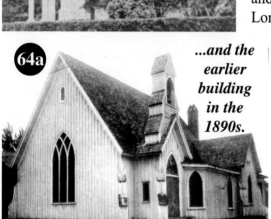

...and the earlier building in the 1890s.

Immanuel Presbyterian Church

Immanuel Presbyterian Church, a mission Sunday school of First Presbyterian Church, began in 1865 in a small shelter on Wooster Street. In 1895, the Wilmington Presbytery formally organized the mission into a church. The Boy's Brigade Club, an institution for underprivileged youth, met daily in the basement of the church "armory" for ten years. A kindergarten also operated there for 25 years. The playground was a popular hangout for the children on the south side of town.

In 1922, a donation from Dr. James Sprunt allowed the congregation to build a brick Colonial Revival-style church and manse. Located at 1103 South Fifth Avenue, the roof of the church was slate and the spire fashioned after that of St. Martin's of the Fields in London, England. Immanuel Presbyterian served the community south of Castle Street until it disbanded in 1969. Some of the congregants became charter members of Emmanuel Associate Reformed Presbyterian Church. The 1922 building was abandoned in the late 1990s. The property owners, the Greater Macedonia Fire Baptized Holiness Church of God of the Americas, saved the beautiful stained glass windows that are incorporated into their new building next door.

Brooklyn & Calvary Baptist Churches

Brooklyn Baptist Church was organized as a mission of First Baptist Church in 1885. By the 1880s the population on the north side of town (Brooklyn) was increasing rapidly, especially among railroad workers. In 1886, the congregation moved into an old building at 714 North Fourth Street. In 1900, a new church building was erected on the site. The Queen Anne-style design was the work of Henry E. Bonitz. The church was painted in two colors: the bell tower, second tower and trim were painted a darker color than the central body of the building.

In 1914, the name was changed to Calvary Baptist Church, because the sectional name did not accurately reflect the current membership, composed of citizens from all parts of the city. In 1919, the building was brick veneered and the towers lowered. At the same time a brick parsonage was constructed on the lot to the south. By 1925, the original membership had grown from 300 to 1,000. In 1955, Calvary Baptist Church moved to North Twenty-Third Street. The old building was torn down in the mid-1960s.

Brooklyn Baptist Church in 1906.

Calvary Baptist Church in 1922. The congregation eventually moved to North 23rd Street.

First Baptist Church

First Baptist Church was an outgrowth of Front Street Baptist Church. As early as 1843, seventeen African-Americans were accepted as members. On November 7, 1864, First African Baptist Church was organized. In the late 1860s, a building was erected on the southeast corner of Fifth and Campbell streets and *African* was deleted from the name. The Wilmington Missionary Baptist Association was organized here in 1883. In 1895, brick veneer was added to the wood-frame church. The beautiful old First Baptist Church was destroyed by fire in 1974. It was replaced by a modern church building in 1977.

First Baptist Church circa 1900.

Shiloh Baptist Church was destroyed by fire in 1955.

Shiloh Baptist Church

Shiloh Baptist Church was organized in 1883 and a wood-frame building was dedicated the next year. By 1911, increased membership caused the congregation to raise funds for a new edifice. The first worship service in the new church was held on January 25, 1914. A spiritual, social and educational center for the neighborhood, the membership was 700 at the time the new church opened. Located at 719 Walnut Street, the Gothic Revival-style brick church had beautiful stained glass windows. Destroyed by fire in 1955, the old building was replaced by a modern one.

Mount Nebo Baptist Church

Mount Nebo Baptist Church was organized in 1911 to serve the community on the south side of Wilmington. Under the leadership of the Rev. George Walter Billips, the first church building was erected at 1000 Wooster Street in 1914. He remained the spiritual leader into the 1940s. A modern brick building replaced the handsome wood-frame one in 1982.

Mount Nebo Baptist Church was organized in 1911.

First Advent Christian Church

The First Advent Christian Church, constructed circa 1870, began as Second Baptist Church. In 1877, the Rev. Joseph Pyram King (1848-1948) was called to serve the church, which was located on the southwest corner of Sixth and Church streets. The Rev. King was ordained a Baptist minister in 1876 and tried by the Eastern Baptist Association in 1880 for preaching heresy. The contentious issue revolved around the Doctrines of Conditional Immorality, in which believers are joined with Christ on the Resurrection Day, and not at the point of death. Likewise, unbelievers are not judged and condemned until the Resurrection day. Despite his dismissal, he continued to pastor his church. In 1895, he founded the first Advent Christian church south of the Mason-Dixon Line, thus the name, First Advent Christian Church. About the same time the church took on its Queen Ann-style appearance. During the Rev. King's 67-year pastorate, he brought thousands of people into the church. Although retired, he gave his last sermon four days before his 99th birthday. He practiced herbal medicine and was well liked in the neighborhoods of south Wilmington. He married three times and upon death had 127 heirs. In 1964, the First Advent Christian Church moved to 2115 S. College Road. Over the years the original building lost one of its towers. The New Jerusalem Missionary Baptist Church has occupied it for many years.

First Advent Christian Church.

First Church of Christ, Scientist

The handsome little Neoclassical Revival-style First Church of Christ, Scientist was constructed in 1907 on the southeast corner of Seventeenth and Market streets. North Carolina's first Christian Science congregation was organized in Wilmington in 1895. Mary Bridgers (1866-1910), a devout founding member, purchased 32 acres of land on Market Street where she developed Carolina Heights, a streetcar suburb. Included in the 1908 plan for the subdivision was a church. She made her feelings known about her religion in

First Church of Christ, Scientist.

the deed for the land that she donated to the church: "...for and in consideration of the love which she hath and bear for the religion of Christian Science, and for the purposes of spreading the said religion." First Church of Christ, Scientist moved to Chestnut Street in 1923 and the old building was sold to Temple Baptist Church. In 1952, the building was destroyed by fire.

St. Matthew's Lutheran Church around 1920.

St. Matthew's Lutheran Church

In 1890, St. Matthew's Evangelical Lutheran Mission Sunday School began in Brooklyn Hall. The next year a wood-frame structure, thirty by fifty-five feet, was built at 919 North Fourth Street. The original building was painted gray-blue and trimmed in white. The interior featured an octagonal oiled tongue-and-groove wooden ceiling. The church was a mission of St. Paul's Evangelical Lutheran Church, founded by German immigrants in 1858. For many years, St. Matthew's was knows as St. Matthew's English Evangelical Lutheran Church to distinguish its English services from the German ones at St. Paul's. The Rev. G. D. Bernheim, D.D. was installed as pastor in 1892 when the church was formally organized. The same year a parochial school building was constructed behind the church.

After 53 years in Brooklyn, St. Matthew's moved to a new building on the corner of Seventeenth and Ann streets. Dedication of the new edifice took place on February 25, 1945. In 1963, the church moved to 1060 South College Road. The old wood-frame church was torn down after the congregation moved out of the building.

Oak Grove Cemetery in the 1920s.

Oak Grove Cemetery

Known as the *poor man's burial ground*, Oak Grove Cemetery began in 1870 when the city purchased property south of Marstellar Street, where Sixteenth and Seventeenth streets are today. Originally called City Cemetery, it was renamed Oak Grove, in 1882, for the beautiful live oaks on the eastern portion of the property. By the 1880s, the original cemetery was full and the city purchased more acreage. A small lodge was erected in 1883. During the first twenty years of existence, 2,000 persons were buried in Oak Grove. They were the working poor and underprivileged. It was the final resting place for city dwellers who could not afford a plot in a private cemetery. Oak Grove was their only alternative, especially after recessions, the Great Depression and the influenza epidemic of 1918-1919.

Although there were some tombstones in Oak Grove, many of the poor could not afford them. They decorated the graves with shells and all kinds of items from their homes, which identified their loved ones. An article in a 1917 newspaper described the cemetery in this way: "Rude, simple and homely ornaments are found on practically every silent heap. Old and tattered toys, dolls, grotesque with the loss of a head or limb, a rusty tin bugle serving as a foot piece; a broken pitcher, with now and then the shattered remains of some culinary receptacle. In one instance is a shaving mug, a hair brush and a pair of scissors. At another is a worn truss, probably emblematic of the disease whose ravages sent some mortal to this spot. A broken rapier is the grim guardian of another. There is scarcely an article found in the ordinary household that cannot be seen here on a grave. Even knives and forks, the kind that are used for dining purposes, are not missing. Medicine bottles, too, take their part, while at one particular spot is a battered tobacco tin."

The cemetery was separated by race. The majority of graves were those of African-Americans. There was also a

Oak Grove Cemetery in 1940.

wilmington: Lost But Not Forgotten

"potters field" section that was fenced off from the rest. The unknown, criminals and indigents were buried there. There were burials in Oak Grove as late as the 1950s. Over the years, some families moved their loved ones to private cemeteries. In 1961, Sixteenth and Seventeenth streets were cut through the cemetery.

Tombstones were taken across the river to a new city cemetery in Flemington, but the bodies were not removed. The cemetery eventually became the property of New Hanover County. In 1984, Bill Reaves documented over 6,000 persons buried in Oak Grove by poring through the old newspapers and going through death certificates, which list the place of burial. He estimated as many as 10,000 persons were buried there. It was concluded that moving this many graves would be financially prohibitive. The area remains a green space within the city today.

A photograph taken by Mr. Reaves in 1940 shows the graves of his grandparents, Richard Martin Reaves, a Confederate veteran, and wife, Mary Eliza Summersett. The small shed is the caretaker's building. Louis T. Moore took the panoramic photograph in the 1920s. The iron bed belonged to Mary Ann Jones, an invalid who was bedridden for many years.

The Chapel at Oakdale Cemetery as it looked in the 1870s. Oakdale is the final resting place of many of Wilmington's prominent and famous sons and daughters.

Oakdale Cemetery

When the railroad was completed in 1840, Wilmington experienced an unprecedented building boom. Some churches had cemeteries and there were a few old public and private burial grounds, but none had much room to expand. Citing space and sanitation problems, a group of businessmen incorporated a City Cemetery in 1852 to be built outside the city limits. Three years later an ordinance was passed requiring the end of interments in town. The organizers were also mindful of a nationwide movement in larger towns to provide centrally located and beautifully landscaped cemeteries. The first interment (1855) was that of six-year-old Annie deRosset, the daughter of the cemetery's first president, Dr. Armand deRosset. From the beginning, the local name for the cemetery was Oakdale. The designation was not officially changed from City Cemetery to Oakdale until a 1901 act of legislature. The cemetery was located on sixty-five acres of high ground, bordered by three creeks, with an entrance at Miller and North Thirteen streets. The organizers of the cemetery held a public auction to pay for the initial laying out of the streets and lots. Besides private lots, there were public grounds and special sections for different groups. A Hebrew section was dedicated in 1855 for the town's Jewish population, and the Ladies Memorial Association dedicated a section for the Confederate dead in 1872. The public grounds were the final resting place for those who did not have private lots, including seamen and other visitors who died unexpectedly while in town. During the Civil War, the Confederate government contracted with the City Cemetery to bury soldiers who died while on duty in the area. Many victims of yellow fever were hastily buried in an area created especially for them.

A Carpenter Gothic-style chapel was built near the entrance in 1871. Small summerhouses and gazebos began to be built throughout the cemetery in the 1870s. The sandy walks and drives were eventually covered with marl and clay, hard enough to be painted white. In 1896, James F. Post designed a new gate and lodge (chapel) at the entrance.

The orientation of the cemetery changed in 1915 when the entrance was moved to North Fifteenth Street. The handsome stone lodge and the gate, no longer needed near the old entrance, were removed. Over the years, the summerhouses were torn down. Three posts from the original gates survive and stones form the lodge from the outer wall of a family lot. The soldier on top of the Confederate Monument faces the old entrance. Many of the drives have been paved, but there are remnants of the old clay and marl walks. The stones and monuments, walls and fences, and landscaping and vegetation are the most visible reminder of the garden cemetery where citizens enjoyed spending the day with their dearly departed.

The Chapel in 1910.

Oakdale's shady lanes in 1905.

Oakdale's main entrance in 1910.

Part Four

Commercial & Office Spaces

Market Street looking west in 1902.

Market Street Trade

Early on, the first few blocks of Market Street constituted the business center of Wilmington. The two most important buildings in town, the market house and the courthouse, were located within the first two blocks and the ferry landing was conveniently located at the end of the street. Businesses located nearby garnered the most trade. The city fathers laid the first wooden sidewalks here. When damaging fires swept this area in 1819 and 1840, wood-frame buildings were replaced with two or three-story brick ones.

Market Street looking east from Front Street around 1910.

The north side of Market Street in 1914.

A post-Civil War census, taken from the 1866-67 city directory, reflects the types of businesses on this stretch of Market Street: 24 dry goods and clothing stores, 9 grocery and liquor stores, 4 boot and shoe stores, 4 druggists, 3 saloons, 3 hardware stores, 2 restaurants, 2 tailors, 2 tobacco and cigar stores, 2 dentists, 2 physicians, 2 law offices, 1 crockery, china and glassware store, 1 photograph gallery, 1 book and stationery store, 1 newspaper office, 1 jeweler, 1 sign painter, 1 confectionary, 1 bakery, 1 auction house, 1 boarding house and 1 hotel.

First floor storefronts were rented. Each year, in October, lease agreements were contracted and merchants vied for more desirable locations. Second and third floors had offices and were often the residence of the workers below. As the town grew, other streets assumed prominent commercial roles, but the first two blocks of Market Street remained important.

The foot of Market Street circa 1915.

The Masonic Hall in 1908.

Masonic Hall & Carolina Hotel

The Gothic Revival-style Masonic Hall (1841-42) was one of the brick three-story buildings built after the 1840 fire. It was the third building constructed to house St. John's Lodge No. 1, A.F. & A.M. From 1842 to 1899, several Masonic lodges used the third floor meeting room. The second floor was a public hall. It was the site of a party given for Henry Clay when he visited Wilmington during his 1844 presidential campaign. When Daniel Webster visited Governor Edward B. Dudley in 1847, a reception was held for the statesman at Masonic Hall. In 1849 a public reception was held at the hall for James K. Polk, eleventh president of the United States. From 1874 to 1895, the Wilmington Library Association leased the second floor. The library, a center for cultural activity, had readings, lectures and other literary programs in the building. The lodge moved to new quarters on Front Street in 1899. The original Gothic Revival facade was removed in 1907. From the beginning, the first floor was rented as a grocery store. The well-known Grocerteria was located there from 1926 to 1962. Troutman's Beauty School of Wilmington was housed in the building from 1963 to 1986. The historic old building was renovated in 1996.

Brothers Robert Barclay Wood and John Coffin Wood operated the Carolina Hotel. Built after the 1840 fire, it was a premier hotel for visitors to Wilmington for many years. Erambert's Drug Store was on the right corner at street level. By the 1880s, it was owned and operated by J. H. William Bonitz. The hotel was demolished in 1912 and replaced by the Victoria Theater.

The Bonitz Hotel (formerly the Carolina Hotel) in 1908.

J.S. McEachern's Feed & Grain, at 211 Market Street.

McEachern Feed & Grain Store

John Scarborough McEachern (1829-1889) ran a feed and grain store at 211 Market Street. He lived over the store with his wife, Emma Garrell (1835-1900), and their seven children, six boys and one girl. He was a founding member of the Wilmington Board of Audit & Finance and the Bellevue Cemetery Company. The store, which had a cast-iron balcony and Corinthian columns, was constructed after the fire of 1840. In the 1890s, the business was operated by sons, Neil Morris McEachern (his two baby daughters can be seen on the balcony) and William Heiden McEachern (standing in front of the building). The store sold hay, corn, oats, flour, meal, pearl hominy and mixed feed for horses and cows.

The Unlucky Corner Grocery Store.

The Unlucky Corner

The northeast corner of Second and Market streets was known as the "unlucky corner." The late Dr. Robert Fales said it was called that because of a string of business failures there. Others have said that the corner was damp and the ground unstable because Jacob's Run ran underneath it. Neither of these reasons seemed to influence Simon Warren Sanders (1853-1915) who operated The Unlucky Corner Grocery Store there for many years. He had a delivery service and was the first grocer in the city to introduce modern appliances for the sanitary handling of products. In 1896, a photograph was taken of the interior of his store for a national advertisement campaign for Chase & Sanborn, the famous Boston coffee house. When Sanders built a new store further up the street (1904) he named it "The Siwasa" for Simon Warren Sanders.

City Laundry in 1945, just after World War II.

City Laundry Company

Founded in 1906, the City Laundry Company was first located in the Odd Fellows building on North Third Street. Within a few years the business outgrew the rented space and an impressive new building was constructed at 22 North Second Street. The laundry, which took up the entire width of the rear of the building, had press machines, a large ironer for "flat work" and a conveyor that carried wash to the drying room. The business offices were in the front of the building and two storefronts were rented out. Laundry received at ten o'clock in the morning was delivered at three o'clock the same day. The laundry catered to hotels in town and at Wrightsville Beach. J. O. Hinton managed the business. The other proprietors were J. H. Hinton, the owner and manager of the Orton Hotel, and E. I. Hinton, the owner and manager of the Seashore Hotel at Wrightsville Beach. The City Laundry building, which has been altered several times, still stands.

City Laundry as it looked in 1912, two years before World War I.

North Front Street

The first block of North Front Street, with its proximity to Market Street, developed as part of the central business district. The blocks further north, however, took some time and effort. North Front Street sits about twenty feet above the river and the topography made it difficult to build there. High ballast stone and brick walls were constructed to literally keep the street from slipping towards the river. One of those walls is still visible from Water Street between Princess and Chestnut streets. Another problem was the Horse Pond, located at Front and Mulberry (Grace) streets, a wet area that was deep enough to accommodate swimmers. By the 1850s, drainage and street improvements made it possible for houses and businesses to be constructed along the entire length of the street.

North Front Street circa 1906.

North Front Street in 1908.

The horrendous fire of 1843 destroyed most buildings from Princess Street to the north end of town, including all of the railroad buildings. After the fire, a building boom consisting of both residences and commercial buildings occurred along the street. After the Civil War, the commercial importance of the street grew exponentially along with the railroad.

Another building frenzy began in the 1890s. Substantial brick and stone, multi-story buildings, replaced houses along North Front. The proximity to the railroad and the port made North Front Street the premier business district and city center by the first decades of the twentieth century. Commercial activity spread onto the cross streets as well.

A glittering night-time view of Front Street, looking south from the post office in 1910.

North Front Street in 1912.

By 1915, there were no empty lots on North Front from Market Street to Red Cross Street. A business census, taken from the 1915 city directory reveals the following businesses: 5 Banks and Savings & Loan, 1 Bakery, 4 Barber Shops, 1 Boarding House, 5 Cafes, 2 Confectionaries, 5 Clothiers, 1 Cotton Exports Office Building, 2 Department Stores, 7 Dry Goods stores, 3 Drugstores, 2 Five & Dime Stores, 4 Hardware stores, 5 Hotels, 2 Jewelers, 1 Marble & Granite Works, 23 offices in Masonic Temple building, 50 offices in Murchison Buildings, 1 Optical Company, 1 Printing Company, 1 Railroad Office building, 1 Shipping Express business, 2 Shoe Stores, 29 offices in Southern Office Building, 2 Theaters, 3 Tobacco & Cigars, 1 U. S. Post Office and 1 Western Union office. Offices on Front Street included realtors, insurance agents, accountants, physicians, dentists, lawyers, and a myriad of other professionals and businessman. The U. S. Post Office had a district courtroom and the district attorney's office on the second floor. Just about any product or service could be acquired on North Front Street. The streetcar, which ran down the center of the street, provided easy access from the railroad depot to Market Street and beyond.

A bustling North Front Street was the center of the downtown business district in 1930.

The Bank of Cape Fear on North Front Street in 1857.

Bank of Cape Fear

The Bank of Cape Fear, chartered on December 17, 1804, was North Carolina's first bank. It had a longer run than most of the state's other antebellum banks, finally succumbing in 1866 due to banking complexities after the Civil War. The Bank of Cape Fear building, located on the first block of North Front Street, was badly damaged by the fire of 1840. John Norris of New York, supervising architect of St. James Church (1839-40), was hired to plan and oversee extensive renovations to the building. The 1857 line drawing of the bank building shows little of the Norris restoration. By the time the sketch was done, Italianate-style renovations had been made to the building. Vents and brackets adorn the cornice and handsome cast-iron porches, much like those on the Latimer House, appear on two sides of the building.

Bank of New Hanover

81a

anking institutions have often had the resources to afford interesting and architecturally significant buildings. Even the smallest country town usually has an impressive bank building. Such was the case when the Bank of New Hanover contacted well-known Philadelphia architect, Samuel Sloan, to design a building for them. This building possessed all the eclectic elements of Second Empire-style architectural design, such as heavy ornamentation and a high mansard roof with dormers. Located on the northwest corner of Front and Princess streets, the building was ready for occupancy in 1873. Several other banks occupied it after 1902. In 1959, the building was categorized as old-fashioned and replaced by the modern five-story Wachovia Bank building. In 2003, Wachovia built a new bank building on the northeast corner of Third and Grace streets leaving the massive former bank building on Front Street vacant.

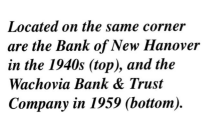

Located on the same corner are the Bank of New Hanover in the 1940s (top), and the Wachovia Bank & Trust Company in 1959 (bottom).

81b

The Wilmington Savings and Trust Company circa 1951.

Wilmington Savings & Trust Company

In 1912, Wilmington had seven banks, all of which were located on either North Front Street or Princess Street. The Wilmington Savings and Trust Company (110 Princess Street) was constructed circa 1910. The contractor, Joseph Schad, also built the eight-story Atlantic Trust and Banking Company building on the northeast corner of Market and Front streets. Schad, a German immigrant, was involved in the construction business in his home country. After moving to Wilmington (circa 1905), his company was employed in the construction of many of the city's most impressive buildings. The Wilmington Savings and Trust Company building was replaced by a parking lot in the early 1960s. The eastern wing of the bank building remains.

Southern Building

A three-story brick dwelling, owned by the McRee family, was torn down in 1904 to make way for a massive new office building called The Southern Building. Matthew J. Heyer (1854-1914) was the entrepreneur who funded the $50,000 business venture. Wilmington architect Charles McMillen designed the building. Porter & Godwin of Goldsboro was the contractor. The five-story structure at 123-125 North Front Street was built of red pressed brick and brownstone. The facade on Front Street was 66 feet wide and the building extended back 115 feet toward the river. All the trusses, beams and girders were steel. The building featured steam heat, electric and gas lights and an elevator. The first floor was designed for two stores. The second through the fifth floors had enough room for 70 offices. The first occupant of the larger of the two stores was The C.W. Polvogt Company. Other memorable stores were the Bon Marche; Anson Alligood, Inc.;

Julian K. Taylor Clothiers; Crawford's Fashion Center and Will Rehder Florist. Real estate companies, attorneys, insurance firms, dentists and doctors rented the upper floor offices. Three Smith family dentists occupied rooms 204 and 205 of the Southern Building for many years. It was an omen when the dentistry moved across the street to the Murchison Building. The building had been a good business address for fifty-years, but it was aging and required extensive repairs. It was razed in 1959 and replaced by a modern bank building.

Matthew Heyer funded the construction of the Southern Building on Front Street in 1904. It was a good office location and shopping hub in downtown for many years.

The Garrell Building and Tide Water Power & Light Company

Henry E. Bonitz was the architect of the Garrell Building (1906), located on the southwest corner of Second and Princess streets. It was made of pressed brick and had limestone trimming. There were two stores on the first floor and offices above. Shortly after construction, the building began a long association with the Tide Water Power Company.

Electric service began in Wilmington in 1886. After twenty years of company buy-outs and mergers, the city's gas, light and transportation companies merged into the Consolidated Railway, Light and Power Company. In 1907, Hugh MacRae organized the Tide Water Power Company, which leased the Consolidated Company. He purchased it ten years later. MacRae's company, of which he held 53% of the stock, had the distinction of being the only public service corporation in the South whose common stock was entirely held in its home town. It passed from his control in 1922

The Garrell Building in 1908.

The Tide Water, Power & Light Company in 1949 (left), and the Tide Water Power Building in 1950 (below).

and during and after the Depression it changed hands several times. It merged with Carolina Power & Light Company (Progress Energy) in 1952. In 1912, Tide Water served 2,300 customers. At the time of the 1952 merger, it served 65,000 customers in Southeastern North Carolina.

The offices of the Tide Water Power Company were located in the upper floors of the Garrell Building from 1907 to 1950 when they moved to a new six story building at the southwest corner of Fourth and Chestnut Streets. It became a New Hanover County office building in the early 1970s. The 1950 building is the only one in the area to have been constructed on Bauhaus principles of architecture. The Bauhaus-style began in Germany after World War I. It veered away from the arts and crafts movement to embrace industrial pre-fabricated functional forms. The shades on the Tide Water Power Building are a particular Bauhaus feature, designed to protect office workers from excessive exposure to heat and glare (form follows function). In 2005, the New Hanover County offices were removed from the building leaving the future of Wilmington's only Bauhaus-style building uncertain.

The Odd Fellows Building in 1907.

The Odd Fellows Building

The Independent Order of Odd Fellows (I.O.O.F.), a benevolent and fraternal organization, was founded in England in the early seventeenth century. The first American lodge was established in 1819, in Baltimore, Maryland. Cape Fear Lodge No. 2, I.O.O.F was organized on January 13, 1842. The group met in several different buildings until 1872 when they moved to a handsome three-story building near the northwest corner of Third and Princess streets. The first floor was rented to businesses. The second floor was rented to another

85b

The Odd Fellows Building in 1967, not long before it was demolished.

fraternal organization, the Knights of Pythias. Odd Fellows Hall was located on the third floor.
A grand new lodge, located one lot south, was erected in 1904. Designed by Wilmington architect, Charles McMillen, the three-story structure was built with Philadelphia red pressed brick and trimmed with granite. The lodge rooms on the third floor had access to the old hall next door. All Wilmington lodges were welcome to use the facility. With its close proximity to the county courthouse many Wilmington attorneys rented office space on the lower floors. The impressive building was razed in 1967 to make way for the Waccamaw Bank (later the RCB Centura Bank) building. The I.O.O.F. moved their headquarters to North Twenty-Sixth Street.

Livery Stables

Early livery companies can be compared to the modern-day gas station, rent-a-car, taxi service, moving company, body repair shop and auto-parts store. Liveries provided an array of services. Their traditional job was boarding and renting horses. They also rented wagons, buggies, hacks, coaches and carriages. If you needed to pick up a friend at the railway station you could rent a vehicle or have the company pick them up for you. If you needed to transfer goods from one part of town to another you could

86b

City Livery Company in 1910.

86a

R.C. Orrell, Livery Sale & Exchange Stables, circa 1910.

rent a wagon or have them do it for you. They specialized in providing carriages for weddings, funerals or other special events. They also sold horses, harnesses, saddles and other horse furnishings. You could purchase a vehicle from them or have it repaired. They were open most hours of the day and night and employed many workers. At any given time there were several livery companies spread across town. The competition kept the cost down and the drivers friendly.

R. C. Orrell, Livery Sale and Exchange Stables, was located on the southwest corner of Third and Princess streets. Built in 1886, the company's proximity to city hall and the county courthouse assured a thriving business.

City Livery Company was located at 108-112 North Second Street. The enterprise was founded in 1870, as T. J. Southerland, Horse Exchange, Hack and Baggage Transfer. In 1901, W. D. MacMillan, Jr., who changed the name to City Livery Company, incorporated the business. Many livery companies went into the automobile business. MacMillan was one of the first to embrace the motorcar and he turned his livery into an automobile sales and services company.

Filling Stations

Incorporated in 1921, MacMillan & Cameron Company was a genuine success story. Partners Henry Jay MacMillen and Bruce Cameron were friends and co-workers at W. D. MacMillan's garage. Shortly after the venture began Henry Jay MacMillan died. His wife, Jane MacMillan, stepped into his place in the firm and was an active partner until 1938.

As more residents purchased automobiles, the demand for gasoline, service and supplies grew rapidly. The first acquisition of MacMillan and Cameron was a curb pump. Next they bought their own tank-wagon to cut down on delivery costs. The firm became wholesalers and was one of the first companies to build and operate a chain of filling stations. In 1939, when they constructed a new

MacMillan & Cameron Co. in 1945.

MacMILLAN & CAMERON CO.

87a

The South's Finest MASTER STATION
WILMINGTON, NORTH CAROLINA
"On the Ocean Highway"

The Gulf Station at Third and Chestnut in 1989, with the New Hanover County Public Library in the background.

building on the southwest corner of Third and Chestnut streets, it had numerous gas pumps, mechanics on duty, a paint shop, electrical shop, motor reconditioning shop, tire sales and service, lubrication equipment and a retail accessory store. The progressive company built a progressive-looking building. The newspaper said, "The building is an ultra-modern edifice, finished in white and blue enamel, with distinctive lines which attract the eye but do not destroy harmony." The Art Moderne-style building, which faced the corner, was stylistically a radical departure from its neighbors on North Third and Chestnut streets.

MacMillan & Cameron was torn down in the early 1970s. The site was used as a parking lot for twenty years until Branch Banking and Trust Company constructed a multi-story office building there.

The service station phenomenon was responsible for the demolition of numerous properties. It was inevitable that the business required the most convenient location, usually a corner lot. An early act of preservation occurred in the 1930s when the site of the Burgwin-Wright House was slated for replacement by a filling station. Fortunately, The National Society of the Colonial Dames in America in the State of North Carolina saved the eighteenth-century house and made it their state headquarters.

When the city expanded into the suburbs, service stations cropped up wherever heavy traffic required them. Twenty-first century self-service mega-stations have everything from convenience stores to fast-food restaurants, but for most of the twentieth century gas stations provided gasoline, oil, supplies and personal service. Oil companies featured unique building designs so the customer visually knew what to expect and fierce loyalties to one company or another developed. Wilmington retains many examples of these twentieth century buildings. Some have cleverly been rehabilitated for new uses, but they are increasingly disappearing from the landscape.

Jewish Merchants

German Jews began arriving in Wilmington in the early 1840s. The majority of them went into the dry goods business. By the latter part of the nineteenth century, many had expanded their retail businesses, some creating wholesale dry goods companies and other large enterprises.

Frederick Rheinstein Dry Goods Company was one of the largest. In 1885, it was reputed to be the leading wholesale house in the state, with a trade of about a half million dollars. Rheinstein was a native of Bavaria, Germany, who moved to Wilmington before the Civil War. During the war he served as a Confederate

The Rheinstein Dry Goods Company on North Front Street in 1910. The architect who designed it, A.S. Eichberg, also designed the New Hanover County Courthouse.

purchasing agent. In 1877, he was elected president of the local Board of Trade. In 1891, Rheinstein built a four-story structure at 216-218 North Front Street. It was constructed of Philadelphia pressed brick and had brownstone columns. The third-floor Romanesque arched windows were ornamented with stone. The architect was A. S. Eichberg of Savannah, Georgia. The building must have been well received because shortly thereafter Eichberg was asked to design the New Hanover County Courthouse (1891-92).

N. Jacobi Hardware Company was a retail and wholesale hardware business. Founded in 1856, Nathaniel Jacobi took over the business in 1869. During the Civil War, Jacobi traveled to Wilmington often for

Nathaniel Jacobi's Hardware Store in 1910.

Charles Finkelstein, Trunks, Leather Goods and Jewelry in the 1920s.

his job as a Confederate purchasing agent. At the end of hostilities, he decided to make it his home. The retail store was located at 10-12 South Front Street. He also owned two warehouses for his wholesale business. One still stands at 9 South Water Street. In 1934, D'Lugins Men's Store moved into the Front Street building. The building was razed after a devastating fire in 1984. The site became a parking lot for nearby businesses.

Eastern European Jews began moving to Wilmington around the turn of the twentieth century. Among them was Charles Finkelstein, who established Wilmington Pawn and Loan Office in 1908. Six years later he purchased a building at 6 South Front Street. The business grew rapidly and in 1917 he purchased the three-story building next door (southwest corner of Front and Market streets). The corner building had been a confectionary as early as 1885. The E. Warren & Son candy and ice cream shop was there for many years.

Charles Finkelstein expanded his South Front Street store into the corner store. He sold dry goods and was especially known for his large line of leather goods. Over the years the building has gone through several changes. In 1918, architect Henry E. Bonitz designed the renovations. During a 1930 remodeling, the cornice was modernized. During the 1950s, fashionable (for the time) metal siding was added to the storefront. In the 1980s, the facade was returned to a more traditional look. At the turn of the twenty-first century, three generations of Finkelsteins have been associated with the landmark store building on the southwest corner of Front and Market streets.

Gaylord's Big Racket Store, Belk-Williams & Belk-Beery

George Oden Gaylord left Beaufort County in 1888, bound for the business world in Wilmington. Twelve successful years later (1900), he built a large department store at 212 North Front Street. The handsome building, designed by Henry E. Bonitz, had a pressed brick facade and red stone trimmings. The first floor was devoted to retail. The second floor had a large millinery department that featured the latest New York styles. Trunks, matting and carpets were sold on the third floor.

Gaylord's Big Racket Store in 1908 (left) and the Belk-Williams Department Store in 1939 (right).

Gaylord's was originally known as the Big Racket Store because of its association with William Henry Belk, whose first department store (New York Racket) opened in Monroe, North Carolina in 1888. Belk stores grew rapidly all across the region but they were not exactly chain stores. They had a voluntary tie that allowed group buying and advertising. Local stores also enjoyed the good reputation of the Belk name.

Belk-Williams opened on November 3, 1915, in the former Gaylord's store. They purchased it in 1918. Belk-Williams founder, J.C. Williams, had trained in the Belk store in Charlotte. By 1926, the store had outgrown its original three-story building. It expanded into the A. David Building across Vance Alley. The two buildings were connected with an overhead bridge across the alley. In 1919, Williams hired W. B. Beery, Jr.,

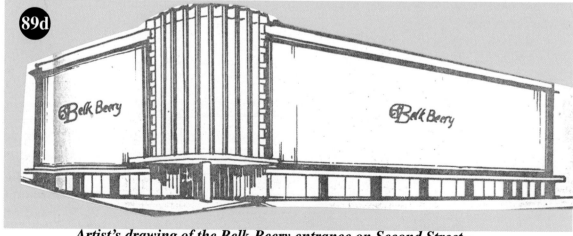

Artist's drawing of the Belk-Beery entrance on Second Street.

Belk-Beery in the 1970s. It now houses the New Hanover County Public Library.

who quickly advanced to the store's assistant manager. When Williams died, in 1943, Beery took over the operation of the business.

In 1946, Belk-Williams became Belk-Beery when a new department store was constructed on the northeast corner of Second and Chestnut streets. The large modern building featured spotlighted merchandise and the first escalator in southeastern North Carolina. The window displays, especially at Christmas, were famous. At the time, shoppers still lived within walking distance of downtown. Teenage girls were known to shop there every day after school. By the late 1950s, shopping centers began popping up in the suburbs. In an effort to make the store more automobile friendly, the department store razed several Third Street buildings in 1965 and expanded its parking facilities. It was inevitable that Belk-Beery would leave downtown as urban renewal took its toll on Wilmington's north side. In 1979, Belk-Beery relocated to Independence Mall.

In 1981, the former downtown department store was renovated as the headquarters of the New Hanover County Public Library. The original store entrance that faced the corner of Second and Chestnut streets was closed and the entrance changed to the east side of the building near the parking lot. The old Gaylord building on North Front Street was occupied by several businesses, including a drugstore. During this time the handsome facade, designed by Henry E. Bonitz, was removed. At the turn of the twenty-first century, the building still stands, but is one of the few buildings left on North Front Street to be renovated.

Efird's Department Store in the 1940's (left). and Einstein Bros. Dry Goods Store in 1910 (below) drew shoppers to North Front Street.

Einstein Bros. & Efird's Department Stores

In 1909, the Einstein brothers (Louis, Adolph, Abe, Edward and Arthur) closed their mercantile business in Kinston, North Carolina, and took the train to Wilmington. Their family had been in Kinston since 1862. They leased the five-story building at the southeast corner of Front and Grace streets that had recently been erected by John H. Brunjes. The Einsteins sold domestic and foreign dry goods and were famous for their large selection of toys imported from Germany. In 1910, they installed the enormous Einstein Bros. signs on top of the building. In 1918 they purchased the building for $80,000.

In 1921, Efird Department Stores, a Charlotte chain, purchased the Einstein Building and spent $25,000 remodeling it. When the store opened on April 10, 1921 it offered five floors of merchandise purchased in New York. Although Efird's had a bevy of New York buyers, it advertised that its owners, the Efird brothers, were Southern born and bred. The Wilmington store, the thirty-first in the chain, hired 125 employees. One of the most popular features was a full service restaurant on the top floor. Claude L. Efird (1902-1976) was the long-time manager of the store, which was extensively remodeled in the 1930s and 1940s.

After more than fifty years as an anchor for downtown retail business, Efird's Department Store closed in the summer of 1975. During the final cleaning, old display cabinets, several ancient office machines and many packing boxes, dated 1906, were found on the fifth floor.

The Five & Ten Cent Store

The S.H. Kress & Co., seen here in 1924, was one of the early five & dimes in Wilmington.

The Masonic Temple building, located at 17-21 North Front Street, was constructed in 1899. The architect, Charles McMillen of Duluth, Minnesota, came to Wilmington for this project. He was a good choice, having already designed and built fourteen Masonic temples. He recognized a growing city and stayed in Wilmington. During his distinguished career, he built many other important buildings. The contractor for the Masonic Temple building was D. Gaetz & Company of Knoxville, Tennessee.

The four-story structure was among the first of many large multi-use buildings constructed on North Front Street during the building boom that occurred between 1890 and 1925. In his design McMillen used pressed brick and brownstone liberally. The third and fourth floor housed the Masonic lodge rooms, a ballroom, parlors, reception rooms and a cafe. About 1920, a small theater was constructed on the fourth floor. The placement of Masonic symbols on the ornamentation indicated the primary reason for the building; however,

S.H. Kress (left) in the 1940s.

Woolworth's (above in a 1949 photo) served customers into the late 1970s.

the Masonic Temple was designed to accommodate other commercial uses. It had retail stores on the ground floor and offices were rented on the second floor.

In 1901, the Masons began a long association with S. H. Kress & Co. When the Five and Ten Cent store opened on June 14, 1901, the newspaper reported that thousands attended the grand opening. The Wilmington store was the fifteenth in the chain and the first in North Carolina. Eventually the store expanded into the entire first floor.

Kress was a fixture on North Front Street for seventy-two years. The downtown store closed in 1973. Buy-Rite moved into the building in 1976. The last department store on North Front Street, it closed in 1989. With a major tenant gone, the fate of the building was uncertain. Fortunately, through the efforts of DARE (Downtown Area Revitalization Effort), a new owner was found in 1992. Movie star, Dennis Hopper, purchased it but major renovations did not occur until 1999 when it sold to a developer. Renamed River City Suites, the building contains retail space and condominiums. The top floor retains its theater and a popular bar is located on the roof.

In 1915, the F. W. Woolworth Corporation leased a three-story Italianate-style building at 110-112 North Front Street. The chain of dime stores had been looking to locate in Wilmington for some time. They chose a location only one block away from their strongest competition, S. H. Kress & Co. Solomon Bear constructed the building in 1880. Morris Bear and Bros. (Isaac and Samuel Bear, Jr.) operated a dry goods store there for many years. The building became rental property after their business dissolved.

In 1938, the store was completely remodeled as the newspaper reported, "from front to back and top to bottom." The new design included an Art Moderne-style facade, an architectural design that became popular after the Great Depression. Incorporated in the new design were different window placements and the cornice was changed dramatically. The facade was remade with stone terra cotta that had a Minnesota marble base.

Exterior trimmings were constructed of stainless steel. Woolworth Corporation architects provided the design that was similar to their other stores throughout the country. Inside, the retail area was expanded to the entire first floor and the soda fountain tripled in size. D. W. Reed, of New York, supervised the construction and R. E. Clarson, of St. Petersburg, Florida, was the general contractor. When completed the store employed 70 workers.

Wilmington lost its only Woolworth store when the business closed in 1978. It was the result of declining trade due to the relocation of the Atlantic Coast Line headquarters to Jacksonville, Florida, and the popularity of suburban shopping malls. The Woolworth Corporation continued to operate the Woolco Department Store at Long Leaf Mall.

Woolworth's in 1918, next to the old post office.

The Woolworth building underwent massive renovations in 1985 but structural problems forced the building into foreclosure after only two years. In 1993, John and Jean Bullock purchased the building. Working with a structural engineer and city inspectors they were able to shore up the building and bring it back to occupancy. "It's good news," said Bob Murphrey, executive director of Wilmington's Downtown Area Revitalization Effort. "What it does is put a good piece of retail action downtown. It's been a long struggle just to get it into good hands and get it started." Renamed, Front Street Centre, the three-story complex contains retail shops, restaurants and offices.

Merchants & Storekeepers

Location was especially important to small stores. Many merchants began in business by renting a market stall or a simple stand on a busy corner. When business prospered they were able to lease a storefront. Storekeepers began the business day by placing their wares out on the sidewalk. Large awnings, many of which reached out to or even into the street, covered the merchandise. In October, when leases were up, there was fierce competition to rent the best-located and equipped buildings. For this reason small businesses moved often. By following their moves in the city directories one can determine the rise and/or fall of their trade.

In his 1988 publication, *Memories Yesteryear*, Dr. Robert Fales wrote, "during the first part of this century, most citizens of the town

The Robbins family at Freimuth's Grocery on N. Ninth Street around 1915.

The Gaston D. Phares & Co. store at 108 Market Street in 1905 (left); Picard's Sporting Goods as it looked in 1949 (right); and at bottom, the Hanby House & Store, built in 1882 on Dock Street. It was renovated in 2003.

believed that, after reaching adulthood, the greatest desire of the average teenager was to own a store or business of his own." Real success occurred when a merchant could afford to build his own building with the name and date of his company proudly embedded in the facade. Wilmington has many such buildings with names of businesses that closed long ago. A building owner had the option of using the space on the upper floor(s) or renting it for extra income. Many lived upstairs until they purchased a house, at which time they could rent to others. It was common for immigrants to live over the store. When family members were brought over from the old country, they were usually offered the upstairs rooms.

Grocery stores were especially adapted for "living over the store." There was a time when grocers could be found in nearly every neighborhood in town. Dr. Fales did a survey of retail grocers from 1902 to 1986: 182 (1902), 222 (1913-14), 168 (1919-20), 207 (1924), 144 (1940), 208 (1950), 150 (1960), 150 (1970) and 102 (1980). Grocery chains and convenience stores begin to show up in the 1960 figures. At the turn of the twenty-first century, only a handful of privately-owned neighborhood stores remain. A few of the neighborhood store buildings have been rehabilitated for other uses, but the majority have decayed or been demolished.

Fourth Sreet, looking north, circa 1910. The Consolidated Market and Firehouse #3 is the building on the right.

Brooklyn and North Fourth Street Business District

It is unknown why the area north of the railroad cut took the name Brooklyn. The designation appears after the Civil War when residential development began in earnest there. In 1869, the *Morning Star* reported, "North of the Wilmington & Weldon Railroad, the population is increasing rapidly and houses are going up in a corresponding ratio." The paper said that as many as seventy-five new houses were constructed within that year. Most of the houses were modest cottages, but along the avenues (Third and Fifth streets) the buildings were two-story dwellings. The mix also included larger, more stylish residences of merchants, preachers, lawyers and other professionals. Within walking distance of the railroad, the majority of Brooklyn citizens found employment there. During the nineteenth century, wooden bridges spanned the railroad cut. By 1874, there were forty-one grocery stores and other small commercial establishments in the area.

Immigrants operated many of the businesses. Brooklyn and North Fourth Street was the "melting pot" of Wilmington. German, Scotch-Irish, Jewish, Syrian, Greek and Chinese merchants lived and worked among the area's African-American population. Due to isolation and dietary concerns, Brooklyn sustained its own meat and produce market.

North Fourth Street became Brooklyn's robust shopping and business district. In the early twentieth century a truss bridge replaced the old wooden one, allowing the streetcar line to extend over it. In 1905, the

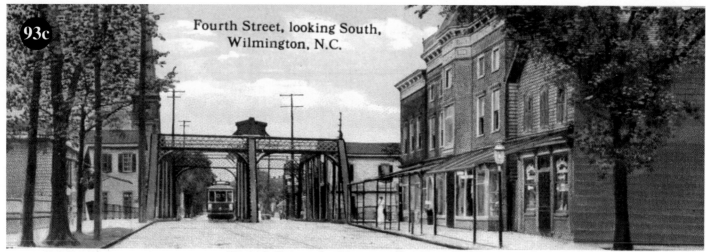

Fourth Street, looking South,
Wilmington, N.C.

Fourth Street, looking south, circa 1915.

area was enhanced with sewer lines and North Fourth Street was paved with brick. Businesses expanded and new commercial buildings were constructed. The J. H. Rehder Department Store tripled in size, with the completion of a three-story addition. The Consolidated Market and Firehouse #3 was built in 1908. Designed by Henry E. Bonitz, the building cleverly provided two essential municipal services.

From 1900 to 1940, Brooklyn and North Fourth Street flourished. Churches and schools were built, expanded and remodeled. After World War II, the area experienced a period of decline as residents began moving to the suburbs. In 1960, employment decreased dramatically when the Atlantic Coast Line Railroad left Wilmington. Buildings were vacated and torn down.

The area was surveyed in 1974 for inclusion in the National Register of Historic Places that recognizes historical, architectural and cultural significance. In 1983, the city issued a bold Plan of Action for the Preservation of the Brooklyn neighborhood. Under the leadership of Harry L. Forden, Jr., the Northside Urban Housing Council, Inc. (later the North Fourth Street Partnership) was formed to assist in revitalization. During the 1990s, the area experienced much rehabilitation and new construction. Continued economic growth is expected in the twenty-first century with plans for a convention center and the corporate headquarters of Pharmaceutical Product Development.

*The Brooklyn Pharmacy in the 1940s (above),
and J.H. Rehder & Company circa 1910 (right).*

94a

The Palace Variety Store at the southeast corner of Fourth and Castle streets circa 1910.

Castle Street & Dry Pond

Researchers have wondered about how Castle Street, which was included in the original town plan, got its name. One theory is that it was named for "Wimble's Castle" which appears on a 1733 rough drawing by James Wimble, the first owner of the property south of Orange Street. Whether he ever built his dwelling there is unknown. Another theory is that it was named for a street in Liverpool, England, the source of many other street names. Wilmington was previously known as New Liverpool (1734-1736). Nun and Church streets ended on high bluffs, but due to Castle Street's gentle slope to the river, it was the site of an eighteenth century landing.

In the nineteenth century the area at the foot of Castle Street was occupied by shipyards, lumber yards, and steam powered sawmills. In the late 1880s, the Wilmington Gas Light Company expanded facilities there. By 1911, the gas company was known as the Tide Water Power Company. Coal-generated electric power

94b

Sixth and Castle streets in 1938.

A steamer docked between Castle and Queen streets circa 1930.

dominated lower Castle Street until 1954, when the Louis V. Sutton Plant was built for Carolina Power & Light Company. Clyde Steamship Company replaced the sawmills in 1913, and Standard Oil Company of New Jersey took over the site in 1942. By 1970, most of the structures associated with these former businesses were either abandoned or destroyed.

In the first decades of the twentieth century, Castle Street developed as the commercial center of south side Wilmington. Dry Pond, a racially mixed working class neighborhood, which derived its name from a former wetland, surrounded it. The Castle Street business district thrived at a time when residents still walked or took the streetcar to shop. Memorable businesses included Palace Variety Store, Golding's and May's Five & Ten Cent stores, Guyton's Food Store, Castle Street Furniture Store, Sidney's Furniture Exchange, Southside and Hall's drugstores, Smitty's Shoe Store, and Friendly, Kotler and Simon's department stores.

By the late 1950s, Castle Street declined as a commercial center due to competition with suburban shopping centers. During the 1960s, 1970s, and 1980s, many of the buildings were left vacant or torn down. Friendly Department Store, founded in 1910, survived until 1995, while several barber shops and Hall's Drug Store (a restaurant) continue to operate.

In an effort to revitalize the former retail corridor, the Castle Street Association was formed in 1994. Castle Street was cleaned up and cleared of crime. During the first few years of the twenty-first century, new businesses and specialty shops give this street renewed vitality. The blocks closest to the river have been added to Wilmington's Historic District and many of the original Dry Pond dwellings have been renovated.

The Tide Water Power Company facilities at the foot of Castle Street in 1950.

Eating Establishments

After the Civil War, Wilmington had four restaurants. By 1915, there were twenty. Hotels and boarding houses also had dining rooms that served locals as well as guests. "Eating out" at lunchtime was generally a male activity during the nineteenth and early decades of the twentieth century. Women and children dined at home except on special occasions. Although some men went home for the noonday meal, cafes and restaurants catered to businessmen and professionals. There was a large concentration of restaurants near the railroad and the courthouse. By the 1930s, lunch counters and cafeterias were popular. In 1950, there were over 60 restaurants downtown.

Located directly across from the Atlantic Coast Line railroad depot, the Atlantic Inn and Cafe catered especially to traveling men. German immigrants, John G. L Gieschen and Henry Gieschen, established the business in 1881. They advertised that their hotel was "conveniently located in reference to all railroads, and parties arriving or departing by train will find them prepared to serve lunch or a meal at short notice." The Crumpler & Scott Cafe was located at 115 South Front Street. The building was constructed in the early 1850s as a residence. The circa 1915 photograph shows the cast-iron vents and second-story porch of the original Italianate-style dwelling. By 1900, the building was converted into a restaurant. W. B. Crumpler and Ira J. Scott ran the cafe from 1915 to 1939. In the 1980s, it became the infamous Portside Lounge where it was rumored that they served beer with a shot of crime on the side. In 1986, much to the relief of its neighbors, DARE (Downtown Area Revitalization Effort, Inc.) purchased the property. Two years later it was sold, with restrictions that the building be renovated.

Many restaurants were owned and operated by Greek immigrants. The peak period of Greek immigration to the United States lasted for about 30 years, from 1891 to 1920. By 1918, Wilmington had 21 Greek-owned businesses, which included twelve confectionaries and six restaurants. The Saffo family, natives of the Island of Icaria, immigrated to Wilmington in 1909. Brothers

The Crystal Restaurant (above) in the 1940s. The Dixie Cafe (below) was on Princess Street in 1957.

The Crumpler & Scott Cafe on South Front Street circa 1920 (left). The Atlantic Cafe, seen below in 1895, catered to railroad travelers.

Vassilios and Antonios opened Saffo's Restaurant at 219 North Front Street in 1918. The business was updated into a modern facility, in 1941, when it moved next door. The transformation, which featured air-conditioning, fluorescent lighting, comfortable booths and a new lunch counter, brought modern dining with old style hospitality to North Front Street.

Greek immigrants also operated the Crystal Restaurant. Mike and Theodore Zezefellis opened the modern facility in 1939. A year later they

Saffo's Down Town Restaurant on North Front Street in the 1940s (left).

advertised a Thanksgiving dinner special—turkey, dressing, cranberry sauce, whipped potatoes, string beans, corn, pineapple salad, buttered rolls, cherry cobbler and a beverage for $.34! There was a private dining room on the second floor that could handle as many as 150 people. Located at 26-28 North Front Street, the restaurant closed in 1962.

As early as 1893, the Dixie Cafe was located at 117 Princess Street. By 1907, the operation was associated with Greek immigrants. In 1940, when the restaurant was fully remodeled and air-conditioned, Chris Rongotes, Jack Morris and John Konetes were the proprietors. A popular restaurant, it was often referred to as the "unofficial headquarters for downtown business and professional men." The Dixie on Princess Street closed in 1977.

The Purcell House as it looked in 1908.

The Purcell House

Built before the Civil War, the Purcell House attained its name in 1868 when Col. J. R. Davis, proprietor of the Mills House in Charleston, moved to Wilmington with a grand design to make it the most elegant hotel and dining facility in town. He remodeled the four-story granite building, formerly known as the Washington House, to suit his needs and added a wing to the rear. For the grand opening, he invited the town's elite businessmen to an extravagant complimentary dinner that was rumored to cost $1,000. It is not known why he chose the name Purcell House. Among the staff who accompanied him from Charleston was a barkeep named Purcell. At the same time, there was an Episcopal minister (sometimes referred to as a physician) by the name of J. B. Purcell living in Wilmington. Whether they were one the same is unknown, but the name Purcell became associated with the building for over seventy years.

William Springer (1846-1926) purchased The Purcell House in 1887. He redesigned the building to house his hardware and agricultural implements business. He remodeled the ground floor to accommodate two stores and refitted the upstairs hotel rooms. Besides a full line of hardware and firearms, the W. E. Springer Company sold the popular line of Buck's cast-iron wood and coal stoves and kitchen ranges. The company supplied the growing truck farming business with farm implements such as harrows, mowing machines and rakes. Springer, a two-time mayor, remained active in the business until his death in 1926. His descendants sold the Purcell House in 1936 to North Carolina Theatres, Inc. In 1940, the building, which still had hotel rooms on the upper floors, was torn down to make way for the Bailey Theatre. The owner of the theatre stated, "we hope with local pride and genuine interest that the citizens of Wilmington will observe the removal of one landmark and the building in its stead a palace of amusement designed to bring pleasure and happiness to the people of this section."

The famous Orton Hotel in 1907.

The Orton Hotel

In 1885, Colonel Kenneth M. Murchison (1831-1904) opened an elegant hotel in the upper floors of the Murchison & Giles building at 109 North Front Street. He named it *The Orton* for his Brunswick County plantation. His intention was to emulate the opulent hotels popular in the North. The first managers, William Bryan Jr. & Sons, had experience in running northern resort hotels and they brought high taste to The Orton. The store of J. W. Murchison, hardware and agricultural implements, was located on the first floor. The second floor contained a luxurious parlor and the hotel office. The parlor floor was covered with fine red Brussels carpet over which were laid Oriental rugs. The furniture upholstery was velvet, brocade and silk and matched the red carpet. A large chandelier lit the oil paintings, cabinet mirror and grand piano. Long lace curtains covered the windows. The dining room had polished cherry tables, comfortable black walnut chairs and a handsome sideboard. The china was imported Dresden. The kitchen contained the most modern equipment of the time. The guest

The Orton as it looked the day after the fire in 1949.

The luxurious interior of the Orton in the 1890s.

rooms, located on the upper floors, were also richly furnished with Brussels carpets to compliment the cherry, black walnut and ash furniture.

After three years of steady business, a larger and very impressive building was erected north of the original structure (1888). This building, with its spectacular two-story porch, was one of the most photographed buildings in Wilmington. The exterior beauty of the structure was matched by interior charm. The proprietor advertised "magnificent furnishings and decorations, in quiet elegance and comfort, with unexcelled management, located in a central location in the heart of the business district, with every modern convenience." An arched opening connected the two buildings, which together housed 100 guest rooms. The ground floor of

the new structure had three doors: a main entrance in the center with gentlemens' and ladies' entrances on either side. The upper veranda was a continuous series of arches with gilded letters, "The Orton," woven into the fretwork. The architect of the building was J. A. Wood of New York, the supervising architect was James Walker and the contractor was J. S. Allen.

Colonel Murchison died in 1904, and in 1905, Joseph H. Hinton acquired the property. Hinton had

Another view of the Orton Hotel, this one from 1918.

worked nearly every job in The Orton from storeroom boy to hotel manager. He remodeled and upgraded the building. Another story was added to both buildings. Among his interior improvements were a high-speed electric elevator and electric lights, running water and telephones in each room. Steam heat replaced coal-burning fireplaces. He also redecorated the lobbies and dining room. At that time there were 160 guest rooms, 85 of them with private baths and toilets. On the American plan, the rates were from $2.50 to $4.00 per day. Under Hinton's management The Orton continued to be a first class hotel, a mecca for salesmen, tourists and the traveling public at large.

The Orton lost its preeminence to the Hotel Wilmington (1914) and the Hotel Cape Fear (1925). By the mid-twentieth century, the building had deteriorated and several stores were housed on the first floor. On January 21, 1949, crowds of local spectators watched the old landmark burn. The fire department rescued thirty guests from the building's famous second floor veranda. Despite the heroic efforts of fire fighters, the brick building, with its wood frame interior walls, burned like an inferno. The cost of the fire, which spread to 6 adjoining buildings, was estimated at $1,000,000. The only Orton rooms to survive were the basement billiards room, dining room and laundry. The Orton Pool Room continued to operate there for many years and the subterranean Orton eventually became a popular pub. In June 2005, the pool room was reinstated.

The Colonial Inn and Colonial Apartments

The Colonial Inn was a first class small hotel when it opened in 1904. Located on the northeast corner of Third and Market streets, it was built for Oscar Pearsall (1849-1925), owner of a wholesale grocery business. Mr. Pearsall personally went to New York to purchase the furnishings. Thad F. Tyler of Wilmington was the builder. He used white hydraulic-pressed brick, manufactured in Wilmington, with red granite trimmings. The cost of the handsome four-story building, including the furnishings, was $35,000. A bus was purchased to ferry guests to and from the railroad.

The Colonial Inn circa 1910.

The building was probably doomed as a hotel due to a constant turnover in managerial staff. In 1915, Mr. Pearsall decided to remodel the building into luxury apartments. J. F. Leitner, a local architect, renovated the building into ten up-to-date units. The original dining room, a five room apartment and one doctor's office occupied the first floor. The second and third floor had family size apartments that featured steam heat, bathrooms and telephones. Smaller bachelor apartments were housed on the fourth floor. The apartment house featured a push-button elevator, the first in southeastern North Carolina. The building was quarantined for two weeks in 1916, when a case of infantile paralysis struck one of the children living there.

Unfortunately, the Colonial Apartments burned in 1962 just before historic preservation efforts began to take hold in downtown Wilmington. Had it survived a few more years, its prime location and beauty would have surely captured the imagination of preservationists.

The Hotel Wilmington circa 1930 (above) and during demolition in 1975 (below).

Hotel Wilmington

World War I spoiled plans to make Hotel Wilmington the tallest building in town. It was supposed to have ten floors, but the wartime scarcity of materials reduced it to seven. Even then, it was an imposing addition to the city skyline when it opened in 1914. White marble tiles adorned the lobby floor and a broad stairway led to hotel rooms on the second floor. Interior columns were sheathed in brown marble. Plate glass and mirrors were in abundance. The rooms were painted white and the birch doors were stained mahogany. Furnishings were chosen to reflect the latest style in hotel accommodations. The dining room became famous for its cuisine. Located across the street from the general offices of the Atlantic Coast Line Railroad, it enjoyed a thriving business. During World War II, the hotel was crowded with soldiers stationed in the area and their visiting families.

The business declined dramatically after the Atlantic Coast Line closed its Wilmington offices. By the 1970s, the hotel was vacant. The fate of the

building was decided by the Wilmington Redevelopment Commission, which debated whether to tear it down or convert it into an office building. They were advised to demolish the building, because it was too costly to renovate, and it had "no great architectural value." A wrecking ball destroyed this structurally sound landmark in 1975.

Hotel Brunswick

The Hotel Brunswick in the 1950s.

In 1891, the YMCA constructed its first building on the northwest corner of Front and Grace streets. The building became privately owned when the "Y" moved to Market Street in 1913. The new owners converted the building into a hotel, which was variously named Carolina Hotel, Southern Hotel and O'Berry Hotel. By the mid-1920s, it became Hotel Brunswick. Over the years, the building was remodeled several times. The major exterior changes included new entrances for the first floor businesses and a more modern look on the street facade cornice. The building was vacated after the general offices of the Atlantic Coast Line Railroad left Wilmington. In 1970, the Wilmington Redevelopment Commission purchased the building. They said the old building was a "detracting eyesore from the new parking deck and Timme Plaza Hotel." The building was razed leaving a huge hole next to what became the Cotton Exchange. In just a few years the other buildings on the block were saved from demolition by creative developers who renovated them into thriving specialty shops, restaurants and offices.

The Timme Plaza Hotel on the riverfront in 1970.

Timme Plaza Hotel

During the 1960s, a modern hotel was a vital component of the city's urban renewal plan for the waterfront. For 225 years, the river had been the center of the city's commercial activity. The new plan looked to the river as the center for recreational activity. The Timme Corporation, a large manufacturing firm located on Castle Hayne Road, built Timme Plaza Hotel, which opened in 1970. The company made heavy industrial material that was used in carpeting, upholstery, draperies, coat linings and cuddly toys. In 1968, the corporation had an annual payroll of $4 million. A heavy contributor to Wilmington's economy, Timme Corporation decided to invest in downtown Wilmington by erecting an eight-story motor inn that contained 156 guest rooms. The entire first floor was dedicated to kitchen facilities, restaurants, a lounge and a large banquet room that could be divided into smaller ones. The second floor contained the lobby that featured an outdoor portico where up to 20 cars could be parked temporarily for registration. A parking area big enough for 240 cars flanked the building. The 4.5-acre site was landscaped and a swimming pool was built on the riverside. Hilton Hotels eventually purchased the Timme Plaza Hotel. As a Hilton, it has been remodeled and expanded and continues to draw tourists and convention business to downtown.

Tourist Cabins, Motor Courts and Motels

The automobile became popular among all Americans after World War I. Whether a trip downtown or a Sunday afternoon drive, the motorcar allowed convenience previously never imagined. As more people purchased cars, vacation travel changed dramatically. Overnight travel required accommodations, and tourist cabins, motor inns, tourist courts and motels filled the void. By the 1950s, motels were the most popular places for the traveling public to stay. The main draw was being able to park your car at

The Azalea Motel at 5307 Market Street in the early 1960s.

the door of your room. Motels were built along busy highways or on the edge of town where land was cheaper than in the inner city. One-story sprawling buildings replaced individual cabins, a home away from home. They had big and sometimes flashy signs to attract motorists. Many motels had attached restaurants, room for a swimming pool and landscaped grounds. Market Street east along the heavily traveled US Highway 17 had a proliferation of popular motels. Early on, motor inns were privately owned and operated. Interstate highways, hotel chains and more cost efficient styles of multi-story construction resulted in the demise of the motel. By the turn of the twenty-first century they were among the most abandoned properties in the country.

The Camellia Court, on U.S. Highway 17, south of Wilmington (right).

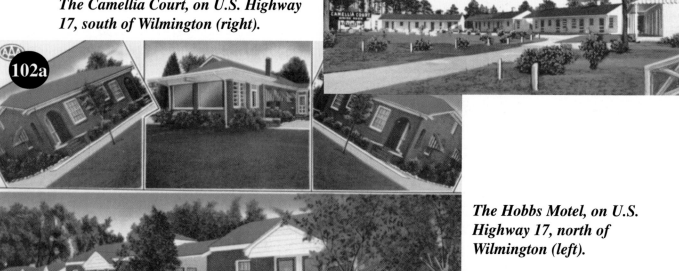

The Hobbs Motel, on U.S. Highway 17, north of Wilmington (left).

Part Five

Wilmington Harbor

103a

Wilmington's waterfront once swarmed with the masts of tall ships from all over the world. This one was docked here in 1895.

Water Street in the early 1900s.

103d

The Historical Waterfront

Wilmington was founded 1739-40, at the junction of the Cape Fear and Northeast Cape Fear rivers, to take advantage of the rivers' economic possibilities. The location provided access to shipping routes along the Atlantic Coast and trade with the interior. The commercial and industrial area that developed along both sides of the Cape Fear River became the engine that drove the economy of the region. Waterfront property was highly valued due to the attached wharves, the center of all shipping activities. Ownership of a wharf, whether public or private, provided lucrative docking fees, leases and rentals. Larger companies generated enough business to fill their docks year-round. Near the wharves were row upon row of warehouses where incoming and outgoing products were stored.

Water Street became the most intensely developed area of town. The street, which was not laid out in the original town plan, was authorized by a 1795 act of the General Assembly. Eventually, the street and a rail line extended from Walnut Street to Surry Street. River-related businesses crowded both sides of Water Street. Ship chandlers sold tackles, blocks, ropes, cordage, sails, cables, chain, paints, oils, anchors and many other provisions and supplies to incoming vessels. At any given time there were thirty to forty commission merchants, who took exports and imports on consignment, and tried to find the

Along the Water Front, Wilmington, N. C.

103c

The Wilmington Harbor circa 1915.

best markets for their disposal. There were several wholesale grocery, hardware, dry goods, ice, furniture and seafood businesses. Auction houses were conveniently located on Water Street. Shipping and insurance agents, as well as produce brokers who dealt in cotton, peanuts, grain, lumber and naval stores rented second floor offices. There were several dealers in coal, wood, brick and shingles. Industrial enterprises included steam sawmills, turpentine distilleries, gristmills, shipyards, breweries, iron works, ice manufacturers, cotton compresses, candy manufacturers, meat packing plants, fertilizer plants and brickyards. Steamship companies carried goods brought in by rail to Atlantic seaports. Railroad companies occupied a large portion of the northern end of the waterfront. Scattered among the commercial and industrial businesses were stables, barrel makers, variety stores, saloons, boarding houses, restaurants and machine shops. The U. S. Custom House and the Marine Revenue Cutter Service (Coast Guard) represented Federal government interests on the waterfront.

Ships from all over the world docked in Wilmington Harbor and gave the city a cosmopolitan atmosphere. Hearing foreign languages and seeing exotic cargo was common. In 1895, the Chamber of Commerce, also located on Water Street, claimed that the "City by the Sea" was the leading trade center of the state. The waterfront was truly the crossroad of that trade.

103b

Water Street in 1905.

J. W. Murchison Company

The J.W. Murchison Company on Chestnut Street in 1939.

The J. W. Murchison Company building was located on the south side of Chestnut Street between Front and Water streets. The business was founded in 1873 as Giles & Murchison. In 1894, Joel Williams Murchison (1853-1926) became the sole owner of the wholesale hardware business. In 1911, he built a large brick warehouse that ran 186 feet along Chestnut Street. The architect was Henry E. Bonitz and the builder, Joseph Schad. It featured an elevator and wide openings where vehicles could enter the building for loading. A wholesale company, it sold to markets both inside and outside of Wilmington and employed many workers. One of the handsomest warehouses in Wilmington, it was torn down in 1965 and replaced by the Water Street Parking Deck.

Hall & Pearsall Warehouse

The Hall & Pearsall Warehouse in 1908.

The Hall & Pearsall warehouse was constructed in 1904 for Oscar Pearsall and Benjamin F. Hall, wholesale grocers. Joseph Shad was the builder. The substantial building was conveniently located between the Cape Fear River and Atlantic Coast Line and the Seaboard Air Line railroads. In the early years the building had large bins where grocery staples were stored until bagged for market. The building, although utilitarian, was built with attractive Flemish bond brickwork. It was one of the last riverfront warehouses when it was torn down in 2000.

C. D. Maffitt Building

The handsome four-story Maffitt building was located on the northeast corner of Water and Princess streets. Architect Henry E. Bonitz designed it for the C. D. Maffitt Ship Chandlery & Supply Company. When built in 1912, it featured an up-to-date wireless station on the roof that provided a constant connection with vessels entering or leaving the port. The Maffitt firm were licensed shipbrokers, customhouse brokers and steamship and vessel agents. They were wholesale and retail dealers in ship chandlery which included provisions and groceries of all kinds, tackles, blocks, ropes, cordage,

The C.D. Maffitt Building in 1914.

sails, cables, chain, paints, oils, anchors and other seaworthy supplies. They sold marine insurance and were agents of the "American Lloyds." For Lloyds they kept records of both American and foreign ships, listing each vessel afloat with full details as to her construction, engines, tonnage, register and owners. Clarence Dudley Maffitt (1873-1958) began his long career in shipping as a cabin boy. He attained the rank of first officer all the while learning how to outfit vessels. The office building and warehouse he built near the waterfront exemplify his success and good taste in architecture.

JoWaHa

The JoWaHa building was an unlikely preservation cause in 1982. The red tin building dominated a prime location just south of the foot of Market Street, and it stood in the center of the $1.1 million federal government funded park called Water Street Plaza. A 1979 structural report had pronounced the over-water building unsound and a nearby restaurateur was leading a fierce campaign to demolish it. While some viewed it nothing more than a ramshackle eyesore, preservationists viewed the old building as link to the once lively commercial and industrial atmosphere that dominated the waterfront for most of its history. The unusual name represented its builder, **Jo**hn **Wa**lker **Ha**rper. It had been empty for several years, since the Stone Towing Company removed their offices when the building's tilt became too extreme. The city thought that a renovated JoWaHa would make a nice visitor's center and the Historic Wilmington Foundation agreed. Charles W. Riesz, Jr., editorial page editor for the *Morning Star*, represented their view when he wrote, "It's red, it's rusty, and it's bent and bashed. It's a survivor from the old days when freight trains rumbled along Water Street past dingy

JoWaHa at the foot of Market Street in the 1960s.

JoWaHa just before demolition in 1982.

warehouses—before we realized that the river was scenic and before Urban Development Action Grants made prettification possible. In the midst of the cleaned-up, painted-up, bricked-up, treed-up Water Street Plaza, the tin building rears its honest red face, the working building on a block of brick gentry." The eyesore theory prevailed, and it was razed in 1982.

Ferries & Bridges

It wasn't until 1929 that Wilmington vehicular traffic could cross the Cape Fear River by bridge. Prior to that time, residents relied upon ferries. The pre-Revolutionary Kings' Highway, which connected the northern colonies to Charleston and points southward, passed through Wilmington to the Market Street Ferry located at the foot of Market Street. Upon crossing the river the traveler had to contend with the boggy, swampy marshland on Eagles Island. From there another ferry took passengers across the Brunswick River. Construction of a causeway across Eagles Island to connect the two ferries began as early as the 1760s. Always an engineering headache, the sinking causeway was in constant need of repairs into the first decades of the twentieth century.

Early ferries were flatboats, towed by rowboats powered by slave labor. There was a bar at the head of the flatboat to keep the horses from tumbling into the river, and another bar at the stern to keep the wagon or coach on board. The toll, which was collected on the east side of the river, allowed customers to cross both

The entrance to the Twin Bridges on the east bank of the Cape Fear River in the 1940s.

rivers and the causeway. In 1907, the first gasoline-powered ferry was put into service. A great improvement, it could ferry fifteen to twenty passengers at a time.

The ferry company was privately owned until 1919, when it was sold to the New Hanover-Brunswick Ferry Commission. With the help of the Corps of Engineers, modern ferry slips were dredged on both sides of the river. In 1920, the commission purchased the *John Knox*, which was named for a Brunswick County commissioner who had encouraged the idea of a joint ferry system. A few years later, the two counties purchased the *Menantic*. With two ferries, twenty-minute round-trip service was established. The *Menantic* was sold in 1933. The *John*

The Market Street ferry to Eagles Island around 1900.

Knox was purchased by the R. R. Stone Company in May 1936. In June of the next year it was caught on a piling and sunk during a storm. The remains were left to deteriorate on the Brunswick side of the river.

Plans to build twin bridges across the Northeast Cape Fear and Cape Fear Rivers began in the early 1920s. One of the original proposals was to construct a bridge at the foot of Ann or Dock streets. Luckily, the location was changed to the northern end of town. The twin bridges were financed by the sale of bonds. Governor O. Max Gardner dedicated them on December 10, 1929. After 189 years of ferry service, citizens could finally cross the river by bridge. A tollbooth was placed at the entrance to each bridge, where a fee was collected to repay the bonds. Payment was completed in 1935, at which time the bridges were made free and the *John Knox* was put out of service. The Isabel S. Holmes Bridge replaced the 1929 structures in 1980. It was named for Mrs. Holmes, a deputy secretary of the Department of Transportation, who promoted the $19 million construction project for her hometown.

The Market Street ferry around 1930, with the JoWaHa Building to the right of the picture (left).

Another view of the Twin Bridges entrance, this one showing the toll booth (right).

The Steamer **Wilmington** *in 1905.*

Steamboats

In 1818, the *Prometheus* and the *Henrietta* became the first two steamboats to navigate the Cape Fear River. The *Prometheus* was short-lived, but the *Henrietta* had a long and profitable life of forty years. By 1825, there were ten steamboat companies in operation. The early steamers were used to carry large cargoes of naval stores products and lumber from upstream to the port. Three types of steamboats evolved: large main-line passenger and freight steamers, small freight boats and tug boats. Competition led to steamboat lines that ran their boats on regular schedules. During the Civil War, the vessels were used to transport troops and supplies.

The *A. P. Hurt*, an iron hull steamer, began service between Wilmington and Fayetteville in 1860. She had six staterooms, thirty-four berths and a freight capacity of four hundred barrels. Owners T. C. and B. G. Worth named her for her first captain. She burned twice and was rebuilt from the hull. The *A. P. Hurt* was one of the last passenger boats to run on the Cape Fear River. On March 7, 1923, she sank at the city wharf where she still remains. With sixty-three years of service, she set the record for longevity.

The legendary steamer *Wilmington* was built in 1881, in Wilmington, Delaware. There was no need to change her name when Captain John W. Harper brought her to Wilmington, North Carolina. She was popular from the time she arrived on April 28, 1891. An iron hull steamer, she was one hundred and thirty feet long, had a beam of twenty-three feet, drew six feet of water and had three decks. The *Wilmington* made two daily runs to Southport. In peak tourist season she carried as many as 2,000 passengers a day. Within an hour she delivered pleasure seekers to a wharf near Carolina Beach. From there passengers would take a little steam-powered train to the beach. Capt. Harper specialized in excursion rates. Institutions, professional organizations, Sunday school classes, and other groups from all over Southeastern, North Carolina rented the boat to take them to the ocean for the day. Capt. Harper had the contract for carrying mail on the *Wilmington*. He also contracted and furnished transportation for the soldiers stationed at Fort Caswell. At one time or another, a large percentage of the population took a trip on the *Wilmington*, making her one of the most beloved vessels in town history.

After the age of steam, she was sold and left Wilmington. In 1960, she was owned by Tampa Bay Excursions, Inc. of St. Petersburg, Florida. Called the *Pinellas,* she was the largest fishing and sightseeing boat on Tampa Bay. On Florida vacations, Wilmingtonians delighted in taking a trip on their old friend. When last sighted, in 1977, she was taking passengers down a river in Brazil.

The *City of Fayetteville* was built in 1902 to compete with the *Wilmington.* She was luxurious. Her staterooms and salons were handsomely furnished and she had running water throughout the boat. Fully electrified, she was a sight to behold after dark. Her owners never profited much from their investment because she was built a little too late to take advantage of the golden era of riverboating. She was carrying a load of cotton when she broke up and sank at the Champion Compress docks in 1913.

The **A.P. Hurt** *(above) plied the waters of the Cape Fear River, as did the* **City of Fayetteville,** *pictured below around 1910.*

Tugboats

*The **Blanch** docked at the riverfront circa 1930.*

Just as the Cape Fear River is the lifeblood of the port of Wilmington, tugboats are the lifeblood of river traffic. They are small vessels, but their looks are deceiving: they are extremely hard workers and are powerful enough to move vessels many times their size. Their job is to assist ocean-going ships as they enter and depart the port or to move much larger barges. In the past, tugboats were constructed of wood or metal-sheathed wood, because the resiliency of a wooden hull prevented damage to both the tugboat and the vessel in berthing operations. Their small size and powerful engines allow them access to all kinds of waterways, and they are tough enough to be called out to sea in rough weather to help a distressed vessel.

Before diesel engines, steam power dominated tugboat design. They were called steam tugs before the term *tugboat* became more popular. The *Samuel Beery*, an early tug, was built in the 1850s expressly for towing and salvaging. From mid-nineteenth century, the Wilmington Harbor was awash with brightly painted tugboats. The business was conducted much as it is today. When a ship approached the mouth of the Cape Fear, a river pilot went on board to guide it through the channel. When the vessel closed in on the docking facility, the tugs went into action, pushing firmly on the sides of the ship, holding her in place, while the ship's crew hustled to secure her position with ropes. Departing ships had to be maneuvered through a 180-degree turn before heading back down river. The completion of the Atlantic Intracoastal Waterway (1932) through Southeastern, North Carolina helped the tugboat business. Tugs were called upon to move barges heavily loaded with freight up and down the waterway. Tugboat crews worked long hours and had to be on call day and night. The tugs were fitted with kitchens and sleeping berths for longer voyages.

The red and black boats of the Stone Towing Company (1895-1982) were moored on South Water Street for decades. In 1982, the defunct company donated their tugs to become part of an artificial reef off Wrightsville

Beach. The reef had been established in the 1960s to attract fish and scuba divers. The *Socony 8*, one of the nation's few remaining steam-powered tugboats, was sunk on December 16, 1982. She and her sister boat, the *Stone Brothers,* were famous for being two of the eleven tugboats that maneuvered the USS *North Carolina* to her berth in 1961.

Preservationists quickly went into action to try to protect the remaining tugs. Unfortunately, the time was not right for preserving a waterfront museum vessel, and no group had the wherewithal to take title. Three more tugboats, *Stone Brothers, Pocahontas* and *R .R. Stone,* were sunk in the Atlantic Ocean. In 1986, the *Estelle Stone,* the last remaining tugboat moored on Water Street, was sold and moved across the river. The Stone Towing Line tugboats were picturesque and reminiscent of the waterfront as a work place.

In the 1970s, an historic tugboat entered Cape Fear history when Thomas H. Wright, Jr., purchased the *John Taxis* for his Chandler's Wharf maritime museum. Built in 1869 in Chester, Pennsylvania, the tug spent most of her working years on the Chesapeake Bay and the sounds of North Carolina. When the boat sank, in 1985, it was lifted out of the water and set on pilings. By 2000, the cost of restoring the old tug was prohibitive and it was demolished in May of that year.

Stone Towing Company tugs docked near the Ice House in 1973.

The tug John Taxis *at Chandlers Wharf in 1985.*

The R.R. Stone *embarking on its last voyage to serve as an artificial reef in 1985.*

Fireboats

The fireboat **Atlantic III** *circa 1960.*

After the devastating fire of 1886, waterfront business owners and city aldermen began expressing the need for a fireboat. The blaze leveled buildings on several blocks around Grace Street and most of the railroad buildings and yards. Several wharves were incinerated because the fire started onboard a steamboat laden with cotton where it quickly spread to the docks.

From 1887 until 1905, the city contracted with a private company to provide fireboat protection. In 1906, the city launched the first publicly owned fireboat, named the *Atlantic I.* It was replaced in 1911 by the *Atlantic II*, which was built in Southport as a shrimp boat, but converted to a fireboat and sold to the city of Wilmington. It was refitted and rebuilt many times until the *Atlantic III* replaced it in 1947.

After 36 years of service the Wilmington *Morning Star* (24 November 1947) felt the *Atlantic III* deserved an appropriate obituary: "Funeral arrangements are pending for the "Atlantic" which is soon to be replaced in active duty by the P-76, a new boat purchased by the city. The old *Atlantic*, veteran of a score of spectacular harbor fires, is survived by her skipper, Captain Charles H. Register. The old hulk will probably be sold for salvage. The final destination of the deceased is unknown, but if sent to Hades, her crew is ready to wager that she can even put out the fire in the infernal regions." The *Atlantic III* was praised for heroism in a 1953 waterfront fire that injured 21 persons and caused huge property losses. The fireboat plunged into the thick smoke and was able to maneuver between two slips where the flames could be pushed away from several warehouses. In 1979, L. G. Thomas of the Wilmington Fire Department said that one of the last duties of the

The **Atlantic IV** *at the foot of Market Street in 1979.*

Atlantic III was to do "What the Japanese couldn't do in World War II: put the *North Carolina* on the bottom." The old fireboat pumped some 135,000 gallons of water into the battleship's ballast tanks to settle it in its berth.

The *Atlantic IV*, a steel-hull tugboat originally named the *T. B. McClintic*, replaced the *Atlantic III* in 1961. It was built in Bath, Maine, in 1932 and had been a floating medical examination room for the United States Public Health Service and a light icebreaker on the Chesapeake Bay. When it was retired in 1986, preservationists tried to find a way to buy it and save it for viewing on the historic waterfront. They were unable to keep it in Wilmington but it was sold to a Brunswick County couple who set about restoring the old tug. Eventually it passed into the hands of other good-hearted preservationists who are continuing the restoration with plans to make it into the area's first tugboat bed and breakfast establishment.

There were two fireboat stations on the waterfront. The first one, built in 1907, stood at the foot of Chestnut Street. In 1926, a two-story fireboat station at the foot of Grace Street replaced it. The station was torn down during urban renewal.

The *Atlantic V* began service in 1986. With four GM six-cylinder engines, the boat is three times as fast as the *Atlantic IV*. With less draft and more horsepower, the fireboat can shoot water a city block and maneuver in low tide.

The Waterfront After World War II

The Wilmington waterfront in the 1950s, as seen from west of Point Peter.

After World War II, Wilmington had fifty-four wharves, piers and docks. Docking facilities could handle as many as sixteen oceangoing vessels simultaneously. However, imports far out numbered exports and Wilmington's status as a port was reduced from an international to a regional level. The major exports at the turn of the twentieth century, naval stores and wood products, had ceased. Cotton, the major export from 1900 through World War I, decreased dramatically. Wilmington became an import distribution center. Molasses and fertilizer production maintained a strong presence, and the Standard Oil Company, which made Wilmington its largest distribution center south of Baltimore, generated most of the business.

In 1960, the Wilmington Harbor still had thirty-nine wharves, but the commercial viability of water-related activities was waning. The State Port Authority was created in 1945. The North Carolina State Docks,

The same waterfront a decade later, in the 1960s.

located south of downtown at the site of the World War II North Carolina Shipbuilding Company, was dedicated in 1952. The rise of the trucking industry, the closing of the Atlantic Coast Line Railroad facilities, the relocation of industry to the suburbs, and fierce competition from heavily state-funded ports in Charleston and Norfolk contributed to the demise of commercial activities on the waterfront. Urban renewal destroyed what was left. The Water Street Parking Deck, built in 1966, was an urban renewal project that focused on bringing shoppers and tourists to downtown.

The waterfront in the 1970s, before the construction of the Timme Plaza Hotel (now the Hilton Riverside).

USS North Carolina

A grand effort to revitalize the waterfront and commemorate World War II began in 1961, when the *USS North Carolina* found a permanent berth on the west side of the Cape Fear River. The battleship had been commissioned on April 9, 1941. It was awarded 12 battle stars for heroic performance in the Pacific. In 1947, it was decommissioned and assigned to the Atlantic Reserve Fleet. In 1958, the U.S. Navy announced the ship would

The battleship **USS North Carolina** *coming home in 1960.*

be scrapped. The next year, James S. Craig conceived the idea to buy the battleship and move her to Wilmington as a memorial to the 10,000 North Carolina men who perished in World War II. The Battleship Commission, under the capable direction of Wilmington native, Hugh Morton, succeeded in raising the funds for the project. On October 2, 1961, the mighty ship arrived. It was taller than a 15-story building and longer than two city blocks. Thousands lined the banks of the river to see the huge ship guided into its berth on Eagles Island. It was opened to the public on October 14, 1961.

Fergus' Ark Floating Restaurant

In 1951, Eldridge Fergus purchased a boat with a concrete hull that had been used from 1946 to 1949 as an office for the Wilmington Reserve Fleet. The vessel was built in Wilmington in 1922. It served as an army troop transport (1920s), a banana boat (1920s), a gambling boat (1930s) and a Coast Guard quarter vessel (1941) before returning to Wilmington. Mr. Fergus converted the boat into a floating restaurant that was moored at the foot of Princess Street. The *Ark* became a popular seafood establishment. A 1950s menu lists a Jumbo Combination Sea Food Platter for $2.50 and Lobster Thermidor for $3.25.

Fergus' Ark, a floating restaurant, was damaged by the battleship as tugs tried to maneuver the World War II behemoth into its berth.

The *Ark* was located across the river from the permanent berth of the USS *North Carolina*, which sailed into Wilmington on October 2, 1961. The most difficult part of navigating the battleship to its Eagles Island resting place was the turn, which had to be made to enter the slip. The river at that point is 550 feet wide and the ship 728 feet long. As the tugboats began to push the battleship into her berth, the bow got stuck in the mud and its stern hit the *Ark* on the port side. The result was a gash in the kitchen wall that caused about $10,000 in

The Ark ended up in Tampa, Florida, where it once again served diners on sparkling water.

damages. Mr. Fergus claimed the *Ark* was the only vessel to be hit by a United States battleship in United States waters. After he repaired the damage, he had a purple heart painted on the point of impact.

A landmark for many years, *Fergus' Ark* was towed away on March 6, 1965. The removal was part of the city's urban renewal program that called for construction of a new Coast Guard docking facility. Mr. Fergus built a modern restaurant on Market Street and the *Ark* ended up on the Tampa, Florida waterfront, as Pappas' Riverboat Restaurant.

Urban Renewal

A decade of decline followed the 1954 decision to move the Atlantic Coast Line Railroad headquarters from Wilmington to Jacksonville, Florida. The incredible loss caused an urgent public and private effort to stop the decline. The result was a $58.9 million dollar new plan for an old city. The idea put forward involved commerce, transportation, public accommodations, education, medical care, highways, care for the elderly and development and preservation of natural resources. By 1965, thirty projects were underway.

Economic growth was the primary function of the newly created Greater Wilmington Industrial Development Committee, Inc., a privately funded group generally referred to as the Committee of 100. They

An artist's conception of the Urban Renewal Project that appeared in the **Star-News** *in 1965.*

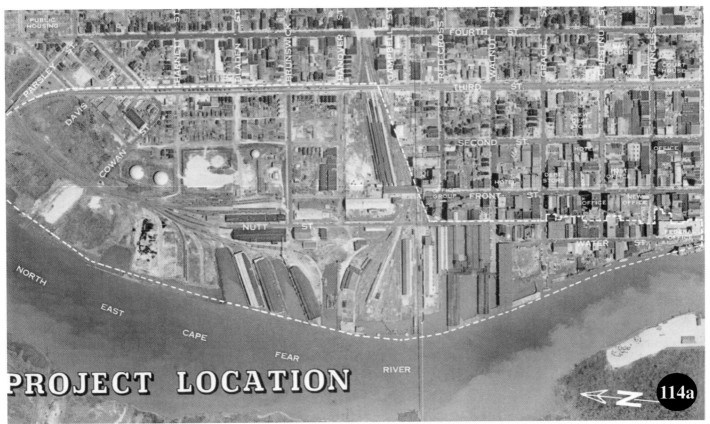

The boundaries of the Urban Renewal Project as presented in 1965.

had great success in attracting new and diverse industries to the area. From 1955 to 1965, seventeen new companies moved to New Hanover County and two local firms expanded.

      Public efforts centered on a bold plan called the Waterfront Urban Renewal Project. The majority of funding for the 3 million dollar plan came from the federal Housing and Home Finance Agency, Urban Renewal Administration. The result was a radical change in way the city viewed the waterfront. For 225 years, the river had been the center of commercial activity. The new plan looked to the river as the center for recreational activity.

The waterfront during the Urban Renewal Project in 1966. The cluster of buildings in the center became The Cotton Exchange. The tall building to the left was the Hotel Wilmington.

The 400 block of North Front Street, demolished during Urban Renewal.

To achieve the goal the city razed all remaining buildings (many had been torn down in the 1950s and early 1960s) on both sides of Water Street from Princess Street to Red Cross Street. Renewal centered around building Cape Fear Technical Institute ($1,075,000), a multi-story hotel ($2,500,000), a parking deck ($635,000) and a new Coast Guard docking facility ($600,000). Site improvements included grading, water, sewer and drainage installations and street rebuilding. Within five years, all of the plans were accomplished. In 1960, after the Atlantic Coast Line vacated their entire premises, the land and buildings were donated to the City of Wilmington. The Waterfront Renewal Project expanded to this property north of Red Cross Street. Plans extended the central business district to the railroad cut and there was talk of building a convention center on the site. The area north of the cut was devoted to industrial development.

The Redevelopment Commission attempted to find new tenants for the railroad buildings, but when this failed the majority of railroad buildings were torn down. They hoped that more efficient one and two-story buildings with ample parking would fill the void. The city's success in urban renewal was contingent on federal funding, which provided two-thirds of the cost. The value of the ACL land and buildings accounted for the city's one-third share of project costs. Urban Renewal, a nationwide program to revitalize and reinvigorate downtowns across the United States, was single-handedly responsible for the loss of most of Wilmington's railroad history and historic waterfront. Forty years later, plans were finalized for a public and private funded complex consisting of a convention center, hotel accommodations and mixed-use business and residential development.

Revitalization

U rban renewal had not reached completion when a strong backlash began to occur among citizens who felt that there was still much to be saved. In 1962, the city established the Board of Architectural Review (later, the Historic Preservation Commission) pursuant to the General Statutes of North Carolina "to safeguard the heritage of the city by preserving any district or landmark therein that embodies important elements of its culture, history, architectural history, or prehistory." The group established historic districts in which they review demolition, relocation of buildings, and exterior changes to buildings and surrounding grounds.

Two private organizations that took the lead were the Historic Wilmington Foundation (HWF) and the Downtown Area Revitalization Effort (DARE). HWF was founded in 1966 to save architecturally significant buildings from demolition. The first organization of its kind in North Carolina, they were especially concerned about residential areas and promoted historic preservation as a way of saving neighborhoods. DARE (now Wilmington Downtown) was founded in 1977 to assist in revitalization of the central business district. They chose preservation of existing buildings over demolition and encouraged owners to turn the upper floors of buildings into residential spaces.

From the beginning, both organizations realized that a vibrant downtown required people living there. Although some buildings were lost, the majority of the projects have been

115a

Adult entertainment clubs were a staple of downtown prior to revitalization efforts.

115b

12 Market Street, saved by Bob Jenkins as Jenkins Interiors, and 10 Market Street, renovated by Charles and Nelda Illick as PIP Printing. Preservation pioneers, they lived over the store.

108 South Front Street, demolished in 1974.

successful, proving that historic preservation enhances the economic well being of the community. As tribute to their vigilance, a twenty-first century visitor to downtown Wilmington cannot imagine the urban blight that existed when these two remarkable organizations were founded.

The Portside Lounge, saved by D.A.R.E. in 1989.

The Cotton Exchange & Chandler's Wharf

The Cotton Exchange before renovation around 1973...

In the mid-1970s, two development projects encouraged revitalization on either end of the historic waterfront. They are credited with bringing businesses, consumers, and visitors back downtown. One was a major rehabilitation of eight crumbling buildings on North Front Street between Grace and Walnut streets. The other recaptured Wilmington's nineteenth century maritime history on a deserted piece of waterfront from Ann to Nun streets.

The Cotton Exchange was the first to open in 1976. It was the creative genius of Joseph Reaves and Malcolm Murray, partners in Harbor Associates, Realtors. They saved eight buildings from demolition at a time when banks were not agreeable to financing downtown ventures. Considerable planning went into turning an empty block of buildings into a unique complex of offices, restaurants and specialty shops. They visited Charleston, Savannah, Atlanta, San Francisco and even Honolulu to learn from similar renovations.

A 1974 fire that gutted one of the buildings hampered the massive undertaking, but they

...and after renovation in the 1980s.

116c

The southern Wilmington riverfront before the construction of Chandler's Wharf in 1972.

utilized every scrap of historic fabric that remained. The interior courtyard and entrance arcade were paved with bricks and cobblestones. An early ballast stone retaining wall, which had originally prevented Front Street from washing into the Cape Fear River, was exposed. The starred heads of hurricane rods inserted after the 1886 earthquake were retained on one of the Nutt Street buildings. Every door, window or other architectural feature was cleaned, repaired and reused. Historic salvage from nearby demolitions was also collected for the project.

The Cotton Exchange, named for a former cotton export company that occupied one of the buildings, was immediately popular with local residents and visitors. During its first full year of operation the North Carolina Preservation Society and the North Carolina Chapter of the American Institute of Architects gave awards of merit to the Cotton Exchange.

Chandler's Wharf, a replica of Wilmington's nineteenth century waterfront, was the idea of Thomas H. Wright, Jr., and William Fetner. In 1978, Wright and his wife, Elizabeth, had already saved more than 30 buildings throughout the downtown.

In the beginning Chandler's Wharf featured simple homes and shops of the time, a warehouse for ship's cargoes, ballast-stone streets, and vintage vessels owned by Mr. Wright. Nineteenth century houses, in danger of demolition, were moved to the site. The one-story brick Iron Works Building was formerly the main office for the Wilmington Iron Works. It was taken apart brick by brick and rebuilt at Chandler's Wharf. A reconstructed warehouse housed a nautical museum. Several vessels were open for tours and the *J.N. Maffitt* took excursions on the Cape Fear River. It was a fun place to dine, shop and learn about Wilmington's maritime history. About the same time Mr. Wright renovated warehouses at the foot of Ann Street and turned them into shops and offices.

In 1984, the museum closed and the building was converted to a restaurant. The last of the vessels, tugboat *John Taxis* was demolished in 2000. The Iron Works building was disassembled and donated to the Historic Wilmington Foundation after Hurricane Floyd damaged it in 1999.

Chandler's Wharf as it looked in the 1980s.

Part Six

Industrial & Manufacturing Sites

Naval Stores and Other Wood Products

An 1855 sawmill located on Point Peter.

The export of naval stores and other wood products made Wilmington an internationally known port-of-call from the early eighteenth century to the end of the nineteenth century. The port had the advantage of connecting Atlantic Coast trade with the extraordinarily rich inland forests.

North Carolina led the world in the production of naval stores from 1720 to 1870. Naval stores products were essential during the age of wooden ships. In *Wilmington, Port of North Carolina*, historian Alan D. Watson described naval stores as "basically consisting of tar, pitch, rosin, and turpentine, derived from the longleaf pine. Crude or common turpentine was the resin collected from boxed, living trees. When crude turpentine was distilled, it produced spirits, oil of turpentine, and a residue called rosin. Burning pinewood in kilns produced tar. Boiling tar in open pits or in iron cauldrons yielded pitch, thicker than tar, but whose consistency depended upon the length of the boiling process. Three barrels of tar produced two barrels of pitch." Turpentine distilleries were abundant. Wilmington wharves were covered with thousands of barrels of turpentine and rosin awaiting transport. The air was redolent with the aromatic odor of pine products.

Dr. Watson defined wood products as "sawn lumber (boards, plank, and scantling), shingles, staves, heading, hoops, hogsheads, posts, oars, masts, spars, yards, and house frames." The most profitable exports were lumber and shingles. The native longleaf pine provided billions of board feet of lumber used in both civil and naval architecture.

In 1855, the Point Peter Sawmill was described in *Ballou's Pictorial Drawing-Room Companion*. The "sawmill presents no other claims

Loading rosin at the waterfront, circa 1872.

for illustration but the fact of its being a prominent object to the eye of the traveler in arriving at or departing from the chief city of North Carolina. Situated at the confluence of the two main branches of the Cape Fear River, it receives its supplies of timber from a great portion of the State, and, having a double water front, the timber is slid directly from behind the saws upon the decks of coasting vessels, which convey it to a market on the Atlantic seaboards. A vast amount is also sent to the West Indies." By 1887, there were seven planing and sawmills, which employed over three hundred hands. Their annual capacity was about forty-five million feet. Cypress trees, which grew abundantly in the swamps of southeastern North Carolina, were second in importance. Cypress wood was used in fencing, water pipes, and framing houses. The most valuable export product made from cypress was shingles.

Loading lumber on Wilmington's waterfront.

The export of naval stores and wood products decreased after the Civil War. By 1900, most of the virgin forests had been depleted.

The Natural Ice Trade

The remarkable history of the nineteenth century natural ice trade includes Wilmington's former Ice House. In 1800, the thought of having enough ice to survive the sultry Wilmington summer was unimaginable. By 1838, advertisements for the frozen delicacy were commonplace in local newspapers.

Frederick Tudor (1784-1864), a Boston Merchant, is credited as the first to bring large scale natural ice supplies to the south. The process of harvesting ice from New England lakes in January and February and making it available in the south in July and August took years to develop. The ice had to be harvested quickly and in large quantities. It had to be stored in the north until summertime. Schooners had to be equipped to handle large

The Ice House is in the middle of this 1925 photograph.

blocks of ice. Finally, once it reached a southern destination, the ice had to be stored until purchased. Most importantly, all these things had to be accomplished with very little melting.

Eventually, the process proved possible. The technology of harvesting ice grew exponentially as the trade increased. As many as 100 men and twelve teams of horses could fill a 25,000 ton New England ice house in very little time. Ice houses, constructed above ground, were insulated with straw and sawdust. Likewise, schooners were fitted with the same insulation. When the precious cargo reached the south, it was quickly unloaded into ice houses built with the same insulating properties.

Filling an ice house in 1872.

William Shaw, a pharmacist, and A. Paul Repiton, a Baptist minister, built the Wilmington Ice House about 1845. Their ice house was located on the north side of Muter's Alley, halfway between South Water and South Front streets. At mid-nineteenth century, Wilmingtonians took for granted summer supplies of ice. Chilled drinks made with crushed ice became very popular. Family gatherings featured ice-cold lemonade. Breweries, which needed continuous refrigeration, could operate year round. Ice carts and wagons made daily deliveries to homes, hotels, saloons and restaurants. Farmers were able to cool their produce, meats and seafood at the market house. The ability to cool perishable foods reduced the chance of disease. Great strides were also made in patient care. High fevers were more treatable when the patient could be cooled down with ice.

The Wilmington Ice House tripled in size during the ownership (1854-1860) of A. H. Van Bokkelen. In 1860, just in time for the Civil War embargo, John E. Lippitt purchased the building and business. After the war, Lippitt's Ice House became the primary dealer in the city. An 1873 advertisement bragged, "Keep Cool. Messrs. John E. Lippitt and Company have now landing two cargoes, consisting of 672 tons of ice, and there are two more vessels on the way to this port, with some 450 tons aboard. Not much prospect of an ice famine this summer."

The natural ice business diminished in 1887 when an artificial ice company opened in Wilmington. Lippitt's Ice House became a Fish and Oyster House. R. C. Fergus & Sons Wholesale Sea Food, who remained there until the early 1990s, purchased it in the late 1940s. During this time the third floor was removed, after a fire destroyed part of the building. On October 6, 1990, a popular beer garden, appropriately named the Ice House, opened in the modern addition to the north of the old ice house. The old building was turned into shops.

Wilmington's 1840s Ice House in 2003...

In 2003, the ice house complex was purchased by Wilmington developers from an out-of-town investor. Despite the efforts of the Historic Preservation Commission, the Historic Wilmington Foundation and numerous citizens, the building was razed on April 26, 2004. At the time of demolition it was the last known antebellum commercial ice house building in the south.

...and demolished by developers in 2004.

Cotton

Cotton exports healed the economic wounds of the Civil War, and with technological improvements, such as the cotton compress, made Wilmington an international cotton-shipping center. Alexander Sprunt & Sons, cotton exporters, was founded in 1866. Scottish born Alexander Sprunt (1815-1884) settled in Duplin County before moving to Wilmington in 1852. When he died, in 1884, he passed the business on to his sons, James (1846-1924) and William H. Sprunt (1857-1939).

The Sprunts were stockholders in the Champion Press Company that opened its compress in 1879. Compresses reduced the volume of the loosely packed cotton shipped from rural cotton gins. The compressed cotton was stored in Champion warehouses. It was also sorted there according to the needs of overseas mills. Eventually the Sprunts took full control of the Champion Cotton Compress and Warehouse. In 1884, they did

Alexander Sprunt & Sons in 1895.

Ships from all over the globe called at the Champion Cotton Compress, like this one in 1910.

about $2 million of business. By 1910, they were the largest cotton-exporting house in the nation. It was reported, in 1912, that Sprunt's exported 500,000 bales of cotton annually. Champion, with its five compresses, produced 5,000 bales a day. Three ships could load simultaneously at the Champion docks. An average of two steamers a week left for foreign ports.

Alexander Sprunt & Sons prospered by getting rid of the middlemen. They shipped straight from the farm to European import houses. William H. Sprunt, well known and respected in the small market towns, was in charge of purchasing. James Sprunt handled overseas sales. The company had warehouses in Liverpool, Bremen, Le Havre, Barcelona and Rotterdam. The business declined during World War I because the lucrative markets in continental Europe were cut off from shipping. Exports dropped dramatically in the 1930s, when competition from Egypt and India forced a national decline in the cotton economy. The handsome brick compress and warehouse complex was demolished during urban renewal.

Sprunt's Champion Compress & Warehouses complex in 1915.

Fertilizer

The Navassa Guano Company in 1910.

In the 1920s, when cotton exports were waning, fertilizer became the mainstay of Wilmington shipping. The Wilmington fertilizer industry began after the Civil War when companies began importing guano, a Peruvian Indian word (huano) that means dung. Guano originally referred to seabird droppings found in enormous quantities on island rookeries and in South America. Wilmington was an excellent location for guano companies. Ships loaded with guano entered the port and left with lumber, cotton and naval stores. Inland farmers needed fertilizer to restore depleted soils. The railroad provided the means to get the commodity to market.

One of the earliest fertilizer factories was the Navassa Guano Company. The smelly factory was constructed in 1869 on the west side of the Cape Fear River where it intersects with the Brunswick River. Eventually the term "guano" became synonymous with any kind of manure. Fertilizer companies imported nitrate of soda, potash, fish, phosphate rock and cottonseed as well as blood and bone from slaughterhouses. A 1912 report stated that the Navassa Guano Company produced 50,000 to 60,000 tons of fertilizer per year. The plant employed 300 laborers and the town of Navassa grew up nearby. Other fertilizer companies of note were Almont Fertilizer Co., Pocomoke Guano Co. and Acme Manufacturing Co. Fertilizer manufacture remained strong in the twentieth century. Eight fertilizer or chemical manufacturers were still in operation in 1965.

Spofford Mills and Mill Village

The *Wilmington Star* reported on January 23, 1900 that, "this time last January the Mineral Spring, two miles from the city, on the Shell Road, was a lonely but pretty spot in the midst of a young long leaf pine forest. The wind sighed ceaselessly through the pine tops and little did the people of Wilmington dream that the scene would soon shift. Industry,

Delgado Mill around 1910.

An aerial view of Spofford Mills and Mill Village, from the 1950s.

however, spread her magic wand over the spring and there has been a change as sudden as it is astonishing. The cognomen of the Mineral Spring has vanished and the Delgado Mill has superseded it. Enterprise and capital has surrounded it with a pretty village of five hundred people and a magnificent $300,000 cotton mill." The textile mill was built for Edwin C. Holt, whose grandfather, Edwin M. Holt, had built the South's first (1837) plaid-dyeing cotton mill in Alamance County. Delgado Mill was named for the younger Holt's wife, Delores Delgado Stevens. The name was changed to Spofford Mills, in 1931, in honor of textile executive George Spofford. In 1933, Wilmington banker, J. Holmes Davis, acquired the mill. When it was sold to Lowenstein & Sons of New York, in 1955, it had 630 looms and 29,408 spindles. The property, which covered more than 100 acres, included 173 dwellings.

Spofford Mills employed 400 workers who lived in the nearby mill village, known as Mill Hill. Besides the dwellings, there was a company store, a swimming pool, a school, a cemetery, a medical clinic, a barbershop and churches. A close-knit community, the residents had their own baseball and softball teams and shared garden spaces. Foreign competition and a declining market led the owners to close the mill in 1967. The imposing brick building was demolished five years later. Several of the mill village houses, office building and the company store remain.

Ethyl-Dow Chemical Company

In 1940, an *Atlantic Coast Line News* article stated that, "one of the most interesting industrial plants to locate in the region is the Ethyl-Dow Chemical Company, which takes bromine out of seawater to be used in making anti-knock gasoline. There were many problems to be considered in finding a suitable location for the Ethyl-Dow plant. There had to be an unlimited supply of clean ocean-water, at some point along the coast where the bromine content was relatively high and where the water was warm enough for this chemical to be extracted feasibly. There had to be some way of discharging the effluent water so it would not 'dilute' the incoming water, an important consideration since there is only about a half-pound of bromine in every thousand gallons of salt water. There had to be facilities for shipping large quantities of acid, alcohol, sulphur and other materials to that plant, as well as for sending ethylene dibromide, the finished product, out to the manufacturing

The Ethyl-Dow Plant in the 1940s...

plants, where Ethyl fluid is compounded for mixing with regular gasoline. Wilmington answered these requirements. Below it, the Cape Fear River creates a peninsula 30 miles long and less than half a mile wide in several places. Locating the extraction plant on one of these narrow spots at Kure Beach made it possible to pump ocean water across the peninsula, into the plant for treatment, then out the other side into the river where it travels a dozen miles before rejoining the Atlantic."

The Ethyl-Dow plant, constructed in 1933, was the first plant in the world to extract an element from seawater. The bromine it produced was essential to airplanes during World War II, when lead was added to gasoline to boost fuel performance. The bromine additive assisted in dispersing the lead out the tailpipe. The plant, which employed about 1,500 people, gave a tremendous boost to the local economy. It was closed in 1945, following the advent of unleaded gasoline. Dave Carnell, a local chemical engineer and Ethyl-Dow researcher, was responsible for the company being commemorated on a North Carolina Highway Historical Marker, which was dedicated in 1993. The plant was demolished, but the ruins remain as an interesting local landmark.

...and as rubble after the wrecking ball.

Part Seven

Leisure Places

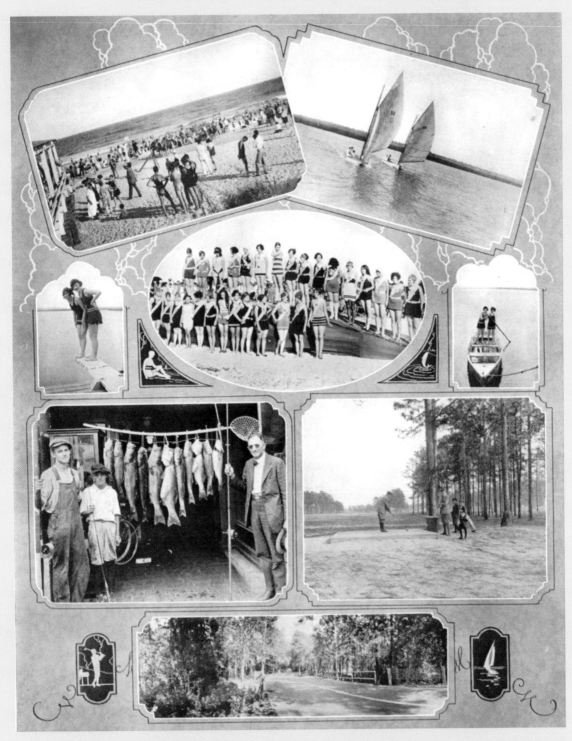

The Bijou, one of Wilmington's premiere theaters, around 1920.

The Bijou

In 1906, Wilmington's first movie theater began in a tent on a plot of ground at 225 North Front Street. James "Foxy" Howard and P. W. Wells, two veteran theatrical performers, formed the Howard & Wells Amusement Company and leased this lot from J. W. Murchison. Into the tent they placed a screen at the western end, sprinkled sawdust on the ground and put in about 300 folding chairs, divided into two aisles. They named their new "theater," the Bijou, which means "a jewel" or "something small and fine." According to author Lewis Philip Hall, "Out in front of the building, Foxy Howard would shout through a megaphone, 'Never out, never over, always going on! Only the high class moving pictures shown. Nothing cheap about it but the price of admission! Only five cents!" This theater is reputed to be the first permanent moving picture theater in North Carolina. From the first, business was very good as the town citizens marveled at the new entertainment. On May 30, 1912, the new Bijou Theatre building opened its doors to the public on the same site. At the cost of $40,000 it was built in the latest vogue in theater construction. Large forty-foot plaster figures adorned the front between impressive ionic pilasters. Over the next several decades, many motion pictures were shown there. Among the most popular were the serials - thirteen week stories that would end each week at a very crucial time, making the audience come back for more the next week. *The Perils of Pauline, Ruth of the Rockies* and *The Trey of Hearts* were some of the earlier ones. Cowboy and Indian movies starring Hoot Gibson, Hopalong Cassidy, Gene Autry and Roy Rogers also played there. By the 1950s, the popularity of television began to reduce movie audiences. On May 29, 1956, the venerable old theater closed its doors for the last time and the building was torn down in 1963. All that remains is a small piece of the colorful tile floor with the name "Bijou" on it. The site became an urban park.

The Royal Theatre, circa 1920.

Royal Theatre

In April 1915, the Howard and Wells Amusement Company bought property on North Front Street between Princess and Chestnut streets, opposite the Post Office. They announced that a new "high class" movie theater, called the Royal Theater, would be built there. B. H. Stephens, a local architect who had also drawn plans for both the Bijou and Victoria Theaters in Wilmington, designed the building. Rhodes and Underwood were the general contractors. The front of the building had pressed brick and terra cotta, with rich decorations. The marquee was lighted with electric lights and featured the name, Royal, in large letters. Around the edges of the sign, rabbits hopped one behind the other. This was the first animated business sign in the city. The "mirror screen" was the last word in projecting surfaces for motion pictures. Made of heavy plate glass, it was the only projecting screen that carried an endorsement from the United States Medical Association. The theater was modernized in 1938 from "top to bottom." The color scheme of blue, black, silver, cream and orange gave the interior an entirely new appearance. The rabbit sign was taken down and beautiful neon signs were added to a new marquee. The building was one of several that were destroyed in the Orton Hotel fire on January 21, 1949.

Victoria~Carolina~Colony Theatre

This theater had several names over its long history. In 1913, the Bonitz Hotel on the northwest corner of Second and Market streets was torn down by Mr. J. M. Solky in order to erect the Victoria Theatre, which, when finished, had a seating capacity of about 1,100. The ample stage had the best lighting in the city. Sunrise, sunset or moonlight could be created by footlights, border lights, bunch and floodlights. There were nine sets of curtains and scenes painted by noted theatrical artisans, Colmer Studio of Washington, D.C. The Victoria not only showed moving pictures, but it was affiliated with B. F. Keith Vaudeville Enterprises. Thus, there were usually live performers on stage. In December 1916, it became a straight motion picture establishment until 1924, when a new management brought back the vaudevillian chorus line of high leg kickers. Other acts presented at the time included tap and soft shoe dancers, solo singers, barber shop quartets, acrobats, jugglers and comedians.

The Colony Theatre in 1962, when children could win prizes like Bingo sets at Saturday matinees...

...and the same building in earlier times, shown here as the Victoria Theatre in 1915.

The advent of motion pictures with sound made dramatic changes in the theater industry. *The Jazz Singer* opened in 1927, starring Al Jolson, and is credited with being the first talking picture, even though there were only three songs in sound. It was not until 1930 that sound equipment was installed in the Victoria. At that time, its name was changed to the Carolina Theatre. In early 1934, the theater was closed for renovation and when it reopened in September of that year, it was the most impressive movie house in the city. The interior had been redecorated in cream and gold. A handsome gold curtain was hung across the stage. Cushioned opera chairs, thick carpets and ushers in tuxedos were added.

In 1954, the theater's management changed again. The Steward-Everett Theatres, Inc., of Charlotte leased the building and the name was changed to The Colony. Edward Marks (1925-1998) became manager of the theater. Mr. Marks was responsible for movie promotions and was well known for his colorfully lighted marquees.

The Colony would welcome scores of movie fans for another twenty years, closing in October 1974 for the last time. Its demise was due to the development of suburban residential areas in New Hanover County, which led to a substantial decline in theater business in the downtown area. The building was torn down in 1975.

Bailey Theatre

In September 1915, George W. Bailey of Asheville came to Wilmington to manage the Academy of Music, the name by which Thalian Hall was then known. He remained in town and in 1939, he purchased the site of the Purcell House at 16-18 North Front Street.

The old hotel was razed and a modern, comfortable and attractive theater was constructed in its place. Mr. Bailey died in July of 1940, a few months before his theater was completed. With a seating capacity of 1,250, the new edifice was named the Bailey in his honor and opened on December 23, 1940. For a number of years, August "Gus" Grist was the manager. First run motion pictures were a staple on the wide screen, the only one in the city. There were two balconies at the Bailey - a lower one for white patrons and an upper one for African-Americans. The Jim Crow era was not over until the 1960s when integration became the norm. The theater advertised as being air conditioned – "always healthfully cool

126b

Front Street's Bailey Theatre in its heyday.

and comfortable." Sometimes though, patrons would swear that they were visiting the Arctic, the temperature was so cold. It was always wise to take a sweater or jacket no matter what the temperature was outside. By the late 1970s, elaborate motion picture palaces in downtowns all over America were losing business. The Bailey Theatre, which had provided such great entertainment for over thirty years, was considered expendable. The last films were run in 1980.

Historic preservationists were distraught when plans to demolish the building for a parking lot were made public in 1983. Attempts to save the unique Art Moderne-style building were unsuccessful but the property owners were convinced to save the Front Street facade and marquee. In the late 1990s, the marquee was taken down after it was deemed unsafe for pedestrians to walk under it.

The Bailey marquee trumpeting Hollywood's latest fare in 1946.

Plantation Club & Jo's Club

Two popular nightclubs in the 1940s were the Plantation Club and Jo's Club. Both were located on Carolina Beach Road. The Plantation Club was located about 3536 Carolina Beach Road or around three miles from the city limits. Owners Abie Rubin and Henry Omirly offered dining and dancing to live orchestra music. During World War II, "Kid" Ellis, a popular former middleweight champion, was the cordial host. The supper club was known as the place to "see and be seen." The waiters wore tuxedos and gambling, liquor and prime steaks were the main fare.

Jo's Club on Carolina Beach Road served good food and good times to servicemen and shipyard workers.

The Plantation Club, which catered to soldiers in World War II, as it was in 1944.

Jo's, located one-half mile south of the Plantation Club, also catered to soldiers during World War II. Owned by J. K. "Bill" Davis, the club was named for his wife, Josephine Mercer Davis. Mr. and Mrs. Davis, who renovated the building, also ran the nightclub. Mrs. Davis worked the cash register while Mr. Davis ran the kitchen. The club, which featured a live band on Saturday night, had room for about 150 diners and dancers. The establishment was known for its stainless steel oyster bar and the tasty oysters that were roasted on site.

The interior of the Plantation Club in 1944, when it offered soldiers, civilians, sailors, marines and airmen good food, tasty drinks and music to fill a dance floor.

The Dairy Queen on Dawson Street in 1998.

Dairy Queen

Dairy Queen is a franchise business that began in Joliet, Illinois, in 1940. Long before Seventeenth Street was made one-way and extended past Marstellar Street, the Eskimo Girl holding the huge ice cream cone was tempting Wilmingtonians of all ages. The creamy, soft ice cream in the cone, topped with a swirl, was a far cry from the familiar hard ice cream that previously had to be chiseled out of a cardboard carton. The Dairy Queen with its unique sign opened on the southwest corner of Seventeenth and Dawson in 1950. The metal sign that was a trademark of the company measured twenty feet long and eight feet high. In 1954, Hurricane Hazel damaged the building, but the sign was unscathed. Clyde Whisenant purchased the business in the 1960s.

Mr. Whisenant sold the property in 1998 and relocated the Dairy Queen to a nearby location. The city sign regulations prevented him from moving the Eskimo Girl to the new location and she was donated to the Cape Fear Museum where she resides with her smile intact.

Miljo Drive In

If you are a local resident of a certain age who attended New Hanover High School in 1950s and 1960s, you probably recall with fondness the Miljo Drive-In. Joe Hines and his wife, Mildred Dixon Hines, brought property at 5213 Oleander Drive in the early 1950s to build the Dixie Pig No. 2, a small barbecue restaurant. When that section of Oleander Drive was widened to four lanes, it took away much of the parking lot for Hines' establishment. After razing the building, they built the drive-in, christened the Miljo from their two first names, farther back on the lot. Around the central building were parking spaces, each with their own menu board and speaker. A canopy sheltered the lot on the east. Over a two-way radio system, customers could order a 15-cent hot dog or a Pizza Burger. A carhop would bring your order to your car and collect whatever was owed. It quickly became a hangout for teenagers, who loved to "cruise the Jo." From a stool near the front door, Mr. Hines kept an eagle eye on all who ventured on his property. As one local remarked, "Joe was the baby sitter for the baby boomers." Radio Station WMFD had a small glassed-in booth near the back of the property. Nightly, disk jockey Bill Weathers would spin current hit records that were requested by customers. The music was interspersed with announcements of high school activities. In 1974, Mr. Hines tore down the Miljo and built Joe's BBQ Barn, which he operated until his retirement in 1986.

Oleander Drive's Miljo Drive-In during the 1950s.

Greenfield Lake and Gardens

Located south of downtown Wilmington, Greenfield Lake and Gardens was once the site of a colonial rice plantation owned by Dr. Samuel Green. The McIlhenny family acquired the property and the lake as early as 1814 and they retained ownership until 1878. During that period, it was called McIhenny's Mill Pond. Around the turn of the twentieth century, this area of New Hanover County began to be developed. The car line was extended from Castle Street first to Third and Greenfield streets and, later in 1913, to "that splendid new development south of the city, called Sunset Park." During World War I, two shipyards were in operation nearby: the Carolina, south of Sunset Park and the Liberty Shipyard at the foot of Greenfield Street. The shipyards attracted many workers who sought employment in Wilmington and the population around the lake grew exponentially.

The Overlake Pavillion at Greenfield Lake in the 1930s.

Greenfield Gardens as they looked in the 1930s.

In May 1918, the Howard & Wells Amusement Company leased the area around the mill pond on Third Street and changed the name to Lakeside Park. Boardwalks, bathhouses, piers, diving boards and various amusements such as a hippodrome were constructed. A zoo that contained several dozen small animals was also installed at the lake. The over-the-lake pavilion was a popular place for spring and summer dances. After the Armistice in 1918, the shipyards ceased to operate and the Howard & Wells Company closed the park.
The North Carolina Sorosis Club, a local women's club founded in 1895, advocated that the City of Wilmington purchase Lakeside Park. Dr. Houston Moore and the then City Commissioner of Public Works, James E. L. Wade took up the cause and finally persuaded the owners to sell the property for $25,000 to the city. The sale was not finalized until 1925.

Commissioner Wade took on the maintenance of Greenfield Park as his pet project and he oversaw the planting of thousands of azaleas, camellias, pink and white dogwoods, wisteria and other flowering shrubs around the lake.

In October 1929, the nation and this region were plunged into the depths of the Great Depression. Hundreds of area residents lost their jobs and quickly became destitute. As part of the Works Projects Administration (WPA), a project to build a five-mile hard surface road around the perimeter of Greenfield Lake was organized to help out these unfortunate workers. Thousands of local workers gave a day's wage, deducted from their salaries, to help pay for the project. About 1,500 men, both black and white, were

Boats on Greenfield Lake in 1915.

hired to construct the road, braving swarms of mosquitoes, poisonous snakes and extreme hot and cold temperatures. By July 1, 1931, Community Drive was completed and it remains a tribute to the spirit of cooperation and compassion that existed in New Hanover County during that trying time.

Near the spillway on Third Street, which controls the lake's water level, is a spring and pump which for many years provided local residents with drinking water. The healthful benefits of this mineral water were widely touted throughout the area.

For a number of years, boats were rented by the public to leisurely row on the tranquil freshwater lake among the cypress trees, draped with Spanish moss. In the spring, when the flowers are in bloom, thousands of tourists from all over the country join local residents in viewing this beautiful municipal garden. Greenfield Lake and Park, a natural jewel enhanced by years of exquisite plantings, continues to be a favorite place for walkers, joggers, bike riders and picnickers.

Cape Fear Country Club circa 1917.

Cape Fear Country Club

In 1896, Col. David Porter Heap, a native of Scotland and Donald and Hugh MacRae, descendants of Scottish immigrants, organized the Cape Fear Golf Club. The first golf course in the county was at Hilton Park, a public park north of Wilmington near the Cape Fear River. The course consisted of seven holes, but could be played for nine, by doubling the first two. The site was shared with a baseball diamond; and, during baseball season, the course was reduced to five holes. It was very primitive, but it predated Pinehurst's first course by about two years.

The first clubhouse was a Wilmington Street Railway System building donated by Hugh MacRae. At about the same time the course was lengthened to nine holes and a new club house was erected, which was a simple cottage in a grove of pines adjacent to the railroad track near the Fourth Street Bridge.

At the turn of the twentieth century, Hugh MacRae's company, the Consolidated Railways Light and Power Company, built a modern electric streetcar system. This opened up the eastern areas of Wilmington to development. Shortly afterwards, the golf club bought fifty-four acres adjacent to the car line near Delgado

Cape Fear Country Club circa 1925 (left), and as seen through the trees on its golf course in 1940 (below).

Mills (later Spofford Mills) just east of the city. The old Hilton clubhouse was moved to a new location on the property. In 1911, the name of the club was officially changed to the Cape Fear Country Club. The club was unique in that it always had female memberships and encouraged their participation in the centuries-old game.

In 1907, the old clubhouse burned and a new one was constructed in a very short time. In 1921, that structure also was destroyed by fire. Leslie N. Boney, Sr., designed the 1921-1922 clubhouse that hosted Country Club members and their guests for over eighty years. That cozy, old, familiar building was razed in 2002, when a large modern facility replaced it.

Donald Ross, a prominent golf course architect, redesigned the eighteen-hole course in 1924 and remodeled it in 1946. It was during the remodeling that all of the eighteen holes were moved south of Oleander Drive.

The Wilmington Athletic Association and the Country Club co-sponsored the Azalea Open Golf Tournament, a regular PGA tour event from 1949-1971. Henry Ransom, the first champion, won $2,000. Almost all of the golfing greats played in the tournament, including Gary Player, Roberto De Vencenzo, Arnold Palmer, Jack Nicholas, Sam Snead, Cary Middlecoff and Tom Watson, in short, a "Who's Who" on the PGA tour of that era.

Masonboro Sound

Adjacent to the Intracoastal Waterway, Masonboro Sound is defined as that part of New Hanover County between Hewlett's Creek to the north and Whiskey Creek (Purviance Creek) to the south. Since before the American Revolution, many permanent residents farmed the rich, dark soil and fished the nearby ocean and creek estuaries. Beginning in Colonial times, prominent Wilmington families would spend their summers on the sound to escape the humidity and heat of the city. William Hooper, Caleb Grainger, Parker

Quince, Oscar Parsley, Dr. James Sprunt and Admiral Edwin A. Anderson, all owned houses here. The extant houses are usually of late Italianate and Colonial Revival-styles with large expansive porches, placed to take advantage of the cool breezes coming east from the ocean across the sound.

One of the early property owners on Masonboro Sound was William Hooper, who was one of three North Carolinians who signed the Declaration of Independence. In 1773, Hooper purchased property on the sound, which he called "Finian." He built a two-story house, which had wide porches on three sides. The foundation pillars were made of hand-made bricks held together with mortar composed of crushed oyster shells. It was the home of Henry and Julia Parsley Peschau when the historic structure burned on March 14, 1931.

In the early twentieth century, Eshcol was the home of Admiral Edwin Alexander Anderson, who was a direct descendant of Dr. Nathaniel Hill, one of the Colonial owners. One of Dr. Hill's granddaughters named the estate, which is a Biblical name meaning "a cluster of grapes." Eshcol seemed appropriate because there were numerous scuppernong grape vines that had flourished on the property since Colonial times. The shingled house was built with two wings, one north and south, the other perpendicular, east and west. A breezeway connected the two. The oldest part of the house was built prior to 1779 and had nine inch floorboards and original doors and hinges. Eshcol was razed in 1963.

In 1873, a summer cottage was built on part of the Oscar G. Parsley property for Jane Parsley Savage and her husband, Capt. Henry Russell Savage. Called "The Wigwam," the one and a half-story frame house was substantially altered by subsequent owners, J. M.

Eschol, the home of Admiral Edwin A. Anderson.

The Wigwam, owned by Captain Henry Russell Savage.

Finian, the Sound home of William Hooper that dated from 1773.

Meditz and Harold F. Dobbins. A one-story hip roof porch, which ran across the entire front elevation, was enclosed in the 1950s. After an attempt to move and save the weather-boarded cottage failed, it was torn down in 2003.

Rice magnate Pembroke Jones' Pembroke Park, Sound Side, in 1915.

Pembroke Park

In April 1902, Pembroke Jones (1858-1919) purchased nearly 1,300 acres on Wrightsville Sound, which would become the nucleus of what became Jones' hunting preserve and lodge. A native of Wilmington, Jones was president of Standard Rice Company, a leading rice shipping firm in the south. He bought additional acreage until the property included more than 2,000 acres. The sprawling land contained pine, hardwood groves, woodland lakes and ponds that were the habitat of prolific wildlife.

As the site for his hunting lodge, Jones chose a bluff that overlooked the tidal marshes of Wrightsville Sound. In 1908, construction began on an Italian style villa, which was designed by J. Steward Barney. It took a year to complete and cost the astronomical sum of $50,000. In the center of the building, a large living room

Pembroke Park's Temple of Love, seen here in 1915, still stands in Landfall. It is the only part of the once grand estate that remains.

The ruins of Pembroke Park in 1972.

was paneled in handsome black walnut and had a high vaulted ceiling. On either end were two massive stone fireplaces with mantels imported from Italy. North of the main room was the dining room, conservatory and kitchen quarters. The south wing contained the guestrooms with bathrooms of marble and tile. Rustic in style, the interior appointments included wildlife paintings and animal skin rugs. However, there were a few furnishings that were more formal, having been imported from Tuscany. An Italian Ambassador, who was once a guest, was quoted as saying that the lodge was "the most perfect note of Italy" in the Americas.

The grounds of the building that Jones called "the bungalow" were landscaped with native shrubs, English ivy and many varieties of flowers. A short distance from the southern entrance of the lodge was the "Temple of Love," which was designed by John Russell Pope (1873-1937), Jones' son-in-law and architect of the Jefferson Memorial. Four pools circled the six-column coquina gazebo. Each pool contained a different kind of fish. The pools were also made of coquina, a building material made by mixing cement with shells from nearby waters. Pembroke Jones entertained the elite of New York and Newport, Rhode Island, society. The Astors, Goulds, Flaglers, and Vanderbuilts were guests at the lodge. There were hunting parties and oyster roasts. Once, an elegant dinner was served on a platform built into the limbs of a huge oak tree, located not far from the lodge. After Pembroke Jones died in 1919, the lodge fell into disuse. In the 1940s, teenagers would lift the chain at the entrance at the end of Summer Rest Road and surreptitiously ride into the woods past the caretaker's house to the old structure. At night, it was a spooky sight. Over the years, vegetation engulfed the main building and vandals carted off the elaborate appointments. The remains of the once elegant villa burned in the summer of 1955.

In the 1980s, development began on the former hunting preserve, which had become the last major tract of land fronting salt water in New Hanover County. The gated community of Landfall, with its golf courses and up-scale houses is located on this property. Only the Temple of Love remains to remind one of its glorious past.

Harbor Island Auditorium

The Harbor Island Auditorium around the end of World War I.

Harbor Island is a low-lying island surrounded by marsh and Wrightsville Sound on the north and southwest and Banks Channel on the east. Originally called the Hammocks, the island was the eastern terminus of the Seashore Railroad for a brief period, until the steam railroad was extended to the beach in 1888. In 1916, the Tide Water Power Company, which owned the railway, constructed a large building called the Harbor Island Auditorium on the island.

Architect Henry E. Bonitz designed the building, which incorporated a sweeping shingled roof into the structure that was capable of seating 2,000 people. At one end, there was a stage that could accommodate large choruses, orchestras and other theatrical endeavors. It was constructed of semi-fireproof material and was heated by gas, which made the building comfortable in the winter. Ventilation was accomplished by rows of openings directly under the eaves. North Carolinians came in droves to the auditorium, where conventions of statewide organizations were held on a regular basis.

In 1927, Oliver T. Wallace and Richard I. Player began developing Harbor Island. Their housing development, called Shore Acres, was very successful and by 1936, the property became more valuable than the auditorium and the building was razed.

A virtually undeveloped Harbor Island in the 1950s.

U.S.O. Club at Harbor Island

The U.S.O. Club on Harbor Island as it looked during the middle of World War II.

As war clouds began to gather in Europe and Asia as a prelude to World War II, a local effort was undertaken to help the national United Service Organization, which brought together six agencies to promote community resources for recreational and welfare activities for military personnel and defense workers. Included under this umbrella were the Y.M.C.A., the National Catholic Community Service, the Salvation Army, the Jewish Welfare Board and the Travelers Aid Association.

In August, 1941, on the northern part of Harbor Island, the Wilmington Salvation Army purchased a building, known as the Pink Club, for the use of the U.S.O. The structure was built in 1930 as a summer annex to the Cape Fear Country Club. The two-story facility was steam heated and had a wide surrounding porch overlooking Banks Channel. There was a pier and pavilion that extended into the water. Two adjacent lots provided parking. A country road (now called Military Cutoff) connecting Highway 17 and the beach area enabled troops stationed at Camp Davis in Onslow County to reach the U.S.O. without having to travel all the way into Wilmington.

The clubhouse received its first guests almost immediately, becoming the first such center in New Hanover County. There were locker rooms, with hot and cold showers, a kitchen and soda fountain, a library, a room for hobby classes and sleeping accommodations. There was a special room where the soldiers could prepare their own fish, caught in the surf or sound. Other activities provided at the site included bowling, roller-skating, motion pictures, music, ping-pong and basketball.

The U.S.O. club closed January 1, 1945 when anti-aircraft training at Camp Davis ended. The property was, for a short time, a private residence before being acquired by the Wilmington Methodist Society for a youth center. The Pink Club was torn down in the 1980s.

Early Lumina

Wrightsville Beach's grand Lumina Pavilion in 1906.

In February 1905, the Consolidated Railway Light & Power Company purchased a large lot at the southern terminus of the beach car line. On this site, the company built a huge pavilion, which cost between $5,000 and $7,000. Designed by Henry E. Bonitz, the building was three hundred feet long and two stories in height. On the ground floor, there was a bowling alley, changing rooms, a ladies' parlor, booths providing cold drinks and lunches, slot machines and other amusements.

It was the second floor that provided the pavilion with its famous dance floor. Local historian, Louis Philip Hall describes the premises thusly, "The second floor was reached by a broad stairway in the center of the building leading to a dance hall 50 x 70 feet, which was encircled by a promenade fifteen feet wide on which

Lumina sunbathers frolic in the ocean-side surf in 1918.

Lumina from the Banks Channel side, circa 1918.

chairs would be placed for the benefit of the spectators." A balcony was placed on the south end of the dance floor to accommodate the orchestra. On the north end of the pavilion was a restaurant with open fireplaces for use in winter.

The large structure took its name, Lumina, from the several thousand incandescent lights used at night to light up the building. The grand opening took place on Saturday, June 3, 1905.

The popularity of Lumina grew rapidly. By 1909, the power company nearly doubled the size of the ballroom. The orchestra was moved from the balcony to an acoustically perfect shell on the western side of the

Virtually all the Big Band greats entertained in the famous Lumina Ballroom, seen here in 1918.

An aerial view of Lumina at the end of World War I.

dance floor, capable of seating twenty musicians. In 1913, another expansion increased the seating capacity to 830 and directly over the porches, a terrace was erected, which was nicknamed the "Hurricane Deck."

During Lumina's long history, almost every famous nationally known dance band played at the "beautiful palace of light." In the beginning, dance etiquette was strictly enforced by chaperones who oversaw rigid Victorian regulations. Rules included no male allowed on the dance floor without proper dress (coat and tie), no intoxicating beverages allowed at any time and no dancing cheek to cheek. All types of popular music were offered, including ragtime, jazz and swing.

Later Lumina

Lumina Pavilion on the south end of Wrightsville Beach during World War II.

The great pavilion reached its zenith in the 1930s when the only way to get to Wrightsville Beach was on the beach car line. Waynick Boulevard was built in the late 1930s and that allowed vehicular traffic onto the beach. In 1939, the Tide Water Power and Light Company sold Lumina to several local businessmen, including Charles Parmele, P. R. Smith and Relmon Robinson. The pavilion looked the same and provided a bathhouse, refreshment stand and amusements on the ground floor. During World War II, dances were held with regularity and featured "named bands." Cab Calloway, Guy Lombardo, Vaughn Monroe and Paul Whiteman were some of the entertainers who played at Lumina.

Lumina as seen from the west side of the island in the 1960s.

After the war, the grand old lady began to visibly decline. Gone were the thousands of electric lights and the declining popularity of the big band sound led the owners to allow a skating rink in what was, in prior years, the famous dance floor, breaking the hearts of thousands of older citizens. In 1954, Hurricane Hazel damaged the building, but failed to completely destroy the old landmark.

In 1962, new management attempted to restore some of Lumina's luster. On the south side of the second floor, a new addition was constructed, nestled under the roof of the old building. Called the Upper Deck, it sold beer and provided set-ups for those patrons, "brown bagging." There was a jukebox and a small dance floor. For a time, it was a popular beach destination. The other part of the cavernous building remained unchanged and private parties were sometimes held there.

By 1973, the magnificent Lumina had fallen into disrepair and become hazardous.

Lumina, a landmark at Wrightsville Beach for generations, came down in May of 1973.

By January 1972, Lumina was badly in need of help. The Board of Alderman of Wrightsville Beach recommended condemnation since the wooden building did not meet the current building code and was considered a safety and fire hazard. The owners were so advised and they decided to try to sell it. A Charlotte group of nightclub owners were very interested in purchasing the property but they were unable to come to an agreement about bringing the building up to code. They decided to invest in a nightclub in Myrtle Beach. In May 1973, the Hooks Wrecking Company began the demolition of the old pavilion, finally ending a magical chapter in Wrightsville Beach history.

Seashore Hotel ~ Ocean Terrace Hotel

One of the earliest hotels on the Wrightsville Beach was the Seashore Hotel, located at Station Three, where the Blockade Runner Hotel is today. Opened on June 15, 1897, the two-story, cream and white frame structure was sixty feet wide with a frontage of 198 feet on the ocean. It was designed by Wilmington architect Henry E. Bonitz. In 1898, the building was almost immediately expanded with an annex of thirty rooms. In 1910, a steel pier, 700 feet long, was constructed on the oceanfront and was connected to the

The Seashore Hotel in 1908.

The famous Steel Pier at the Seashore Hotel in 1910.

hotel veranda by a wide boardwalk. At the ocean end of the pier was a two-story pavilion and observation deck. When the pier opened, fish were caught on hand lines because rods and reels had not become popular at Wrightsville. The pier was badly damaged by a series of nor'easters in 1919-1920 and the remaining pilings were swept away by a particularly strong storm in 1921.

      Fire destroyed the Seashore Hotel on June 26, 1919. A new three-story hotel was erected on the same site, opening in 1922. It retained the old name and offered the guests a large lobby, a ladies' parlor and an elegant dining room on its first floor. The upper floors contained single and double rooms with baths. In 1935, Mrs. J. A. Snyder leased the Seashore Hotel and changed the name to the Ocean Terrace Hotel. Hurricane Hazel heavily damaged it in 1954. About a year later, the old structure burned to the ground.

The Ocean Terrace Hotel, which burned down circa 1955.

The Blockade Runner Motor Hotel as seen in a photo taken by Hugh Morton in 1965.

The Blockade Runner Hotel

For a decade after Hurricane Hazel, there was no large modern hotel on Wrightsville Beach. Community interest in correcting this situation resulted in the local Chamber of Commerce contacting Lawrence C. Lewis, Jr., of Richmond, Virginia. The old Seashore Hotel site was available as there was nothing on the lot except the brick foundations. Mr. Lewis hired Oliver and Smith, architects, of Norfolk, Virginia, to design a seven-story brick structure, containing one hundred and twenty rooms, each one with a view of either Banks Channel or the Ocean. The Blockade Runner Motor Hotel opened on March 22, 1964. The name was chosen in honor of the vessels that slipped past the Federal ships blockading the port of Wilmington during the Civil War.

Hotel Tarrymore ~ Oceanic Hotel

In 1905, the Hotel Tarrymore was constructed by W. J. Moore of Charlotte, just north of Station One on Wrightsville Beach property that ran from the ocean to Banks Channel. The large wooden structure contained one hundred and twenty-five rooms with all of the modern conveniences including private baths, telephones and electric lights. An artesian spring well supplied good, fresh water for the hotel's guests. There

The Hotel Tarrymore on Wrightsville Beach in 1908.

The Oceanic lights the night at Wrightsville Beach in 1924.

were billiard and pool tables, a bowling alley, a saloon, a large bathhouse, card parlors and a large ballroom. The cuisine was considered outstanding.

In 1911, Hotel Tarrymore was sold and expanded. At this time, two wings, with wide porches, were added. The entrance was changed from the center of the building to the southwestern corner where an elegant Queen Ann-style tower was erected. The name of the hotel was changed to the Oceanic. Quickly, it became one of the social centers of the beach. A fine orchestra would play dinner music in the dining room. After the dinner hour, the musicians would often board the beach cars and go to Lumina to play for dances. On Banks Channel, the hotel maintained a small pavilion and dock, where boats or launches were docked. These boats took guests out into the ocean through Moore's Inlet at the northern end of the beach. The grand Oceanic Hotel burned in the big fire of February 28, 1934, which destroyed everything on the Northern Extension except two cottages.

The Oceanic as it looked in 1930. It burned to the ground in the great fire of 1934, along with virtually everything else on the north end of Wrightsville Beach.

Carolina Yacht Club

Carolina Yacht Club, organized in 1853, as it looked in 1910.

On April 24, 1853, a group of seven gentlemen from Wilmington met to organize the Carolina Yacht Club, which is the second-oldest yacht club on the east coast. They wanted to race their yachts on Banks Channel and in the Atlantic Ocean. The nearby beach, later to be known as Wrightsville, was one of a chain of barrier islands that spans the coastline of North Carolina from Virginia to the South Carolina line. A small structure was built on the beach mid-way between the ocean and the sound, beside Deep Inlet, which then bisected the island, just to the south of the present club site. By August 1897, a larger one-story building, with a wide surrounding veranda, had replaced the smaller club facility. On November 1, 1899, this clubhouse was destroyed by a very strong hurricane.

The next year, a two-story structure with spacious upper and lower porches was erected on the site. The first floor had a large all purpose room, with the second floor devoted to a men's lounge and a bar. The two one-story wings that extended out on either side of the main building toward the sound contained the bathhouses, one on the north for women and one to the south for men. A large canopy was built over the car track, where members boarded the beach cars. A boardwalk was built over the marsh to Banks Channel, which had a dock for members' boats. This building was completely destroyed by Hurricane Hazel in 1954 and a similar replacement facility was completed in 1955.

Hanover Seaside Club

Organized in 1898 by immigrants from the Province of Hannover, Germany, the first clubhouse was located on Carolina Beach. At that time, roads were so poor from Wilmington to the Federal Point peninsula that a trip to the beach necessitated a ride on the Steamer *Wilmington* down the Cape Fear River. A small train, called the *Shoo-fly* met the boat, which provided transportation to the beach.

By the spring of 1906, an electric railway had been constructed from Wilmington to Wrightsville Beach. The beach cars made the round trip to the beach in about an hour, cutting down the traveling time tremendously. Therefore, in May, 1906, the club acquired a lot on the southern extension of Wrightsville Beach, just a few blocks north of Lumina. Designed by club member Henry E. Bonitz, the clubhouse opened on September 3,

The Hanover Seaside Club building at Carolina Beach in 1910.

The Hanover Seaside Club at Wrightsville Beach, built on a lot purchased in 1906 (left). The building burned in a December 1981 fire that took the life of one firefighter and seriously burned another (below).

1906, with elaborate fanfare. The clubhouse at Carolina Beach, though damaged by a hurricane on September 17, 1906, was sold to Thomas F. Boyd in 1909.

The 1906 clubhouse was a three-story frame structure with broad verandas on each floor. Bathhouses, a bowling alley, kitchen, dining room, a card room and a ladies parlor occupied the first two floors. On the third floor were fourteen rooms, which were rented to club members during the summer season. The entire structure was lighted by electric lights.

The rambling clubhouse served as the members' summer home for seventy-five years. In the wee hours of the morning of Sunday, December 6, 1981, the old wooden building was completely destroyed by fire, leaving nothing but the western facade standing. A new clubhouse, designed by Conrad B. Wessell, Jr., was dedicated in time for the 1983 season.

Sunbathers next to Johnnie Mercer's Pier in the 1950s.

Johnnie Mercer's Pier

O nce known as the Atlantic View Fishing Pier, the wooden pier was located at the eastern end of Salisbury Street on the northern extension of Wrightsville Beach. In the 1940s, a bait and tackle shop occupied the base of the pier that extended 912 feet out into the ocean. Later, the shop was relocated onto the pier where admission tickets and beachwear were available. Souvenirs sold there included almost anything made of shells, often with letters spread over the item spelling out Wrightsville Beach in large letters.

The snack bar sold hot dogs and french-fries, whose cooking odors intermingled with the salt air. Pinball machines and pool tables were nearby. The pings and clickedy-clack of the ongoing games combined with the gentle roaring of the waves to assault the ears.

Johnnie Mercer's Pier stretches out into the blue Atlantic in a sparsely developed Wrightsville Beach strand in 1961.

Before the berm was completed in 1966, it was possible to park right on the beach. Many day-trippers used this area as their beach headquarters and a lifeguard, provided by the Town of Wrightsville Beach, made them feel safe. The pier also provided shade on sunny days. Restrooms and changing rooms were readily available.

Before the advent of air-conditioning, the beach was a popular destination for town folks who wished to cool off on a summer evening. A beach drive usually included a visit to the pier to see what the fishermen were catching. Pier walking required keeping a good distance away from a fisherman who was casting his line. It also involved praising or celebrating a good catch.

Fishing piers are notoriously vulnerable to nature's fury and this pier was no exception. It was completely destroyed in 1954 by Hurricane Hazel and was often damaged by subsequent storms. In 1996, Hurricane Fran destroyed the wooden pier. A concrete replacement was opened in 2003.

Johnnie Mercer was the genial host and owner for a number of years. He would greet old timers and newcomers as they purchased their tickets while listening to thousands of whopping fish tales. Tragically, Mercer was killed in an automobile accident near McCumber's Station in 1964. After his death, his family sold the pier, but the name has been retained.

Shell Island Resort in 1924, one of New Hanover County's two beaches for African-Americans.

Shell Island

Moore's Inlet separated Shell Island, located north of Wrightsville Beach, from the beach until the 1970s. The inlet was navigable and boats from the Oceanic Hotel took guests out into the ocean for fishing trips and sight seeing excursions. In the mid-1930s the inlet began gradually to fill in.

In 1923, the Shell Island Resort was established as a recreational area for African-Americans. L. T. Rogers, a white contractor, built a large pavilion and boardwalks on the island. The R. R. Stone Company operated a gasoline boat known as *Stone No. 5*, which made four-round trips daily across Moore's Inlet to the

Shell Island in 1960.

Shell Island Resort suffering from erosion in 1997.

island. It was very successful and the Tide Water Power Company made plans to extend the beach car line from Harbor Island to the resort.

Music was very popular at the resort as jazz was performed nightly at the pavilion. Local musical clubs and orchestras were frequently featured during the summer months. Tragically, the resort was completely destroyed by fire in 1926 and it was not rebuilt.

The island remained uninhabited until the mid-1960s, when the land on Wrightsville Beach became scarce and extremely valuable. In winter of 1965, Moore's Inlet was completely filled in to allow vehicular access to the island. Immediately Shell Island began to develop. In 1986, the Shell Island Hotel Resort, a multi-story condominium and hotel complex, was built on the northern end of the island. When the 169-unit resort was constructed Mason Inlet was a half-mile away.

During the mid-1980s, Mason Inlet, which divided Shell Island and Figure Eight Island, started a slow migration to the south. By 1996, the inlet had moved 3500 feet until it was within 100 feet of the Shell Island Hotel Resort. After several requests by the resort, permission was obtained to install sandbags as a temporary barrier to keep the water from coming into the resort. Several attempts to get approval from the North Carolina Coastal Resource Commission for a permanent hardened wall were denied.

In 1998, the Mason Inlet Preservation Group was formed to seek a solution to the problem of the migrating inlet. They quickly agreed that the only practical action would be to return the inlet to its original location. Thus began a four-year project that necessitated getting permits and approvals from various federal and state agencies and the New Hanover County Board of Commissioners. The dredging began in December 2001 and was completed when the new inlet was opened on March 7, 2002. The old Mason Inlet was closed on March 14, 2002.

The original Station One concession stand at Wrightsville Beach.

Station One at Wrightsville Beach

In the early part of the 20th Century, Wilmington was connected to Wrightsville Beach by a beach car line owned by the Tide Water Power Company. The first stop on the beach after it crossed Banks Channel was called Station One. A small station with open sides greeted each visitor as the train made the wide turn south to the ultimate destination of Station Seven - the famous dance pavilion, Lumina.

Just to the north of Station One was the massive hotel first known as the Tarrymore and, later, the Oceanic, a property that ran from the ocean to Banks Channel. In 1925, a large two-story wooden building was erected on the channel side of the boardwalk at Station One. This was the Channel View Hotel. Located on the ground floor of this building was Pop Gray's Soda Shop, which quickly became a popular hang out for area teenagers. For nearly twenty years, Earle Eugene Gray, a native of Randolph County, NC, was the genial proprietor. On the east side of the tracks at a junction of the boardwalks was Bud Werkauser's stand, a small open air structure painted battleship gray, which competed for customers with Pop Gray. Although the Channel View Hotel and Gray's Soda Shop did not succumb to the big 1934 fire, the businesses had to close. When new structures were built, Pop opened a drug store north of Station One, which he operated until the close of World War II.

The town docks at Station One in 1959.

Mr. and Mrs. Lester Newell moved to Wrightsville Beach in the late 1920s. They ran the concession stand that was owned by the Tide Water Power Company at Station One. After several years, the Newells bought the drink stand and sandwich shop, which was a simple open-sided wooden stand with fold-up sides. From these modest beginnings, Newell's became a Station One retail mecca for over fifty years, finally moving into a large modern brick building in the early 1950s. The store sold canned goods, staples, hardware items, gifts, souvenirs, novelties, toys, bathing suits, towels, suntan lotion, shovels and pails, beach chairs, etc. There was always a soda fountain in one end of the store. The business was sold in 1976, and again, in 1992, when it became part of a national retail chain named Wings.

In the distant past, not far from the Station One business district were family cottages of the Bears, the Sternbergers and the Vollers. All are gone now, replaced by a high-rise condominium, built in the mid-1970s, appropriately called Station One.

Newell's Department Store at Station One in the 1940s.

Beach Cottages

For the better part of the twentieth century, it was virtually unheard of to live year around on the beach. There were a few hardy souls who seemed to ignore cold, breezy temperatures and remained on the strand during the winter, but for most area residents, the beach was a place to move to around Memorial Day and to leave for town on Labor Day.

An early Carolina Beach cottage circa 1900.

When the beach cars were the only way to get on Wrightsville Beach, the men of the family would take the train to and from the city each weekday morning and evening. The ladies and children would spend the day staying cool and playing in the sand. Early on, while the men were working, it was about the only time that a lady would hike her skirts to wade in the sea. It was not until the mid-twenties that bathing suits for women, as we know them, existed. Even in the 1930s, letters to the editor of the *Star-News* frequently railed against the indecent women's bathing attire seen at the beach!

At Carolina Beach, as well as Wrightsville, summer cottages were simple structures, built of inexpensive materials, usually of wooden shingles or siding. On the ocean front, the plain, spacious cottages would be built on pilings, which would allow ocean water to move freely underneath during a storm or an abnormally high tide. Shutters over windows, hinged at the top, would be propped open by a single stick to allow shade in the boiling summer sun or to be secured tightly when there was a severe storm. The first floor of cottage, opposite the waterside, would often be encased in latticework, allowing an opening for children to enter to play in the sand on a rainy day. Wide porches were a characteristic feature, containing wooden rocking chairs. They would facilitate evening conversations with near neighbors or strollers along the boardwalks.

This Carolina Beach cottage, lot and land sold for a whopping $850.00 in 1920.

Mrs. W.H. Northrop's Wrightsville Beach cottage in 1911.

The interior furnishings were as simple as the architecture. Cot-like beds were sometimes placed on porches in hot weather in order to catch some breath of air. Wicker furniture was very popular at the beach. Many can remember the childhood agony of a bad sunburn, intensified by sitting on bumpy wicker. In the kitchen or bathroom, there was the distinctive smell of brackish tap water. It stained the sinks and tubs a bright yellow or orange. Drinking water was usually brought from town.

In the 1970s and 1980s, the simple cottages with their large porches began to disappear. By the turn of the twenty-first century, property values soared at both Wrightsville and Carolina Beaches and multi-story condominiums and large private homes on tiny lots have replaced the old cottages. Fortunately, the Wrightsville Beach Museum is housed in an old beach cottage. It may eventually be the only one left.

Beach cottages line both sides of the beach car line bisecting Wrightsville Beach around 1915. By the 1980s, the quaint dwellings began to give way to larger, modern beach houses and condos.

The Ocean Inn at 115 South Lumina Avenue on Wrightsville Beach in the 1930s.

Beach Inns and Guesthouses

Not everyone could afford or enjoyed staying in the big hotels on the beach. Some families, particularly with small children, liked spending their vacations at the smaller guesthouses or tourist homes, which were once common on both Wrightsville and Carolina Beaches. Most of the inns were big frame two or three story cottages with no more than twenty rooms. They rarely had private baths. Usually, there was one communal bath on each floor. Some of these establishments had dining rooms, which were locally known for their tasty meals. All had wide porches, where guests could sit in rocking chairs, particularly in the evenings, to soak up the salt sea air.

The Kitty Cottage at 104 South Lumina Avenue in the 1940s.

The Carolina Inn, at Carolina Beach, as it looked in 1945.

A successful inn or guesthouse could guarantee that their customers would come back year after year. Most vacationers would book the same week or weeks each season. There are very few of these hospitable accommodations left, because the real estate they are on is vastly more valuable than the business it supports, and most vacationers prefer better-equipped condominiums.

The Wanda Inn & Rooms, at 4 North Lake Park Boulevard in Carolina Beach, as it was in 1963.

Carolina Beach

Carolina Beach's famous Shoo-Fly train circa 1910.

Carolina Beach is located on the Federal Point peninsula, which is bounded on the west by the Cape Fear River and on the east and south by the Atlantic Ocean. Like its sister beach, Wrightsville to the north, Carolina Beach was hampered by the lack of good access roads. A trip by horse and buggy would take the better part of a day. In the late 1800s and early 1900s, the best way to get to the area was to take the steamer *Wilmington* from its dock at the foot of Market Street, and cruise down the Cape Fear River. A small train, called the *Shoo-fly*, met the steamer at its dock and transported passengers over to the beach. The New Hanover Transit Company was instrumental in promoting the development of the beach. By the end of the first decade of the twentieth century, summer residents were building cottages, guesthouses and hotels.

On the oceanfront, the Carolina Beach Pavilion was built about 1884 by Captain John W. Harper, owner of the steamer *Wilmington*, as part of his oceanfront hotel complex. The building burned in 1910 and was replaced by the Carolina Moon Pavilion, which was destroyed by fire in 1940, along with twenty-four other businesses in the immediate vicinity.

Carolina Beach Pavilion in 1907.

APPROACH TO CAROLINA BEACH, N. C. BY STATE HIGHWAY 40

148c

The highway to Carolina Beach in the 1930s.

Development increased when roads to the peninsula improved. A new road, designated as State Highway #40, as it neared Carolina Beach, followed the same route as present Dow Road and then onto Cape Fear Boulevard to the ocean.

Several hotels were built to take advantage of the new highway that was completed in 1929. The Ocean View Hotel opened in 1930. It was located on the oceanfront between Harper Avenue and Carolina Avenue North. The same year, James R. and Florence Ludwig Bame opened the red brick, three-story Bame Hotel on Cape Fear Boulevard. It became one of casualties in the big fire of 1940. Rebuilt on the same site, it reopened in the summer of 1941. This hotel was razed in 1976. W. C Fountain, an oil distributor from Wilmington, built the Hotel Royal Palm in 1936. The name was changed to Hotel Astor in 1983. A fire destroyed the old hotel in June 2005.

148d

The Ocean View Hotel in 1932.

Two landmark hotels from Carolina Beach's World War II era, the Hotel Bame in 1942 (above), and the Hotel Royal Palm in 1940 (below). Renamed the Hotel Astor in 1983, the Royal Palm was destroyed by fire in 2005.

Greer's Motel catered to an increasingly mobile population that emerged after World War II.

After World War II, there were many small motels and guesthouses, built on what became known as Pleasure Island. They were usually operated as a "mom and pop" businesses. The Greer Motel was an example of such an enterprise. The family "owned and operated" atmosphere of the beach began to change dramatically in 2005 when the price of land on the beach skyrocketed and the Carolina Beach Board of Aldermen began allowing construction of multi-story buildings in certain areas where it had formerly been prohibited.

The boardwalk has been a part of Carolina Beach since its very earliest days. Along the boardwalk at various times were bowling alleys, bingo parlors, dance halls, miniature golf courses, souvenir shops and arcades. Cotton candy machines spun out the pink confection and salt-water taffy was available for those who like the sweet, chewy substance and did not mind the chance of a broken tooth or crown.

By the 1930s, a Ferris wheel and hobbyhorses or merry-go-round were located just off the boardwalk. Sea Shore Amusement Park added the Octopus and bumper cars during World War II. Later, the Moon Rocket and Bullet thrilled stouthearted visitors. At one time, there was a chair ride over the ocean near one of the

Seaside Amusement Park drew crowds of fun seekers in 1946.

The famed Carolina Beach Boardwalk in 1962.

fishing piers. In the 1970s, the amusement park moved from its traditional site near the ocean and boardwalk to a place just south of Snow's Cut Bridge. Known as Jubilee Park, it was the last of these carnival-like parks on Carolina Beach when it closed in 2005.

The same boardwalk filled with soldiers, civilians and bathing beauties in 1945.

Illustrations

Most of the illustrations in this book can be found in the North Carolina Collection at the New Hanover County Public Library (NHCPL). Images from other collections are noted by the name of the owner. All chapter page photographs are taken from City of Wilmington, North Carolina. *Prepared by E.G. Stellings & Co., Wilmington, N.C., circa 1930. The photographs were taken by Louis T. Moore when he was secretary of the Wilmington Chamber of Commerce from 1921 to 1941.*

20. Kenan House
    20A NHCPL
21. Greek Revival-Style Townhouses
    21A NHCPL ~ *Frank Leslie's Illustrated Newspaper*, 1865
22. P.K. Dickinson House
    22A NHCPL
23. James Dawson House
    23A NHCPL
24. Mrs. Davis' Boarding House
    24A North Carolina Collection, UNC-Chapel Hill
25. Robert H. Cowan House
    25A NHCPL
26. John L. Holmes House
    26A NHCPL
27. MacRae's Scottish Castle
    27A NHCPL
    27B NHCPL
28. The Drs. Thomas House
    28A North Carolina Collection, UNC-Chapel Hill
29. Bellamy & Sprunt Houses
    29A NHCPL
    29B NHCPL
    29C NHCPL ~ *Star-News*
30. Springer House
    30A NHCPL
31. Vollers House
    31A NHCPL

Part Three: Community Spaces
    NHCPL
32. U.S. Post Office, Built 1888-1891
    32A Bellamy Mansion Museum
    32B NHCPL ~ Gift of Mary Vail Lanier
    32C NHCPL ~ Gift of Mary Vail Lanier
33. Post Office Park & Woodrow Wilson Huts
    33A NHCPL
    33B NHCPL ~ Louis T. Moore Collection
    33C NHCPL
34. 1844 U.S. Custom House & Alton Lennon Federal Building
    34A NHCPL ~ U.S. Customs Photograph
    34B NHCPL
35. Market Houses
    35A NHCPL
    35B NHCPL
    35C NHCPL

36. Wilmington Railroads
    36A NHCPL
    36B Cape Fear Community College
    36C Bellamy Mansion Museum
    36D NHCPL - Gift of Henry Von Oesen
    36E NHCPL
37. Bluethenthal Field
    37A NHCPL ~ Gift of Lucille Blake
    37B NHCPL ~ Louis T. Moore Collection
    37C NHCPL
    37D NHCPL ~ Randy Allen Collection
    37E NHCPL
    37F NHCPL
38. Seaman's Bethel
    38A NHCPL
    38A NHCPL ~ Louis T. Moore Collection
39. Marine Hospital
    38A NHCPL
    39B NHCPL ~ Allegood Collection
40. City Hospital
    40A NHCPL ~ *NC Medical Journal*, May 1891
41. James Walker Memorial Hospital
    41A NHCPL
    41B NHCPL ~ Gift of Terry & Tanya Dubberly
    41C NHCPL
42. Community Hospital
    42A Cape Fear Museum
    42B NHCPL
43. Harper's Sanitarium
    43A NHCPL
    43B NHCPL
    43C NHCPL ~ Bill Reaves Collection
    43D NHCPL ~ Bill Reaves Collection
44. Babies Hospital
    44A NHCPL ~ Louis T. Moore Collection
    44B NHCPL
    44C NHCPL ~ Beeler Collection
45. YMCA
    45A NHCPL
    45B NHCPL
46. Ruth Hall
    46A NHCPL
47. Boys Brigade Armory
    47A NHCPL
48. Williston School
    48A NHCPL

48B NHCPL
48C NHCPL ~ Louis T. Moore Collection
48D *The Willistonian*, 1966
49. Tileston School
  49A NHCPL
  49B NHCPL
50. Union School
  50A NHCPL
  50B NHCPL
51. Hemmenway Hall
  51A NHCPL
52. Isaac Bear School
  52A NHCPL
  52B NHCPL
  52C NHCPL
53. James B. Dudley School
  53A NHCPL
  53B NHCPL ~ Beeler Collection
54. Wrightsboro School
  54A NHCPL
55. Academy of Incarnation
  55A St. Mary Church Archives
56. St. James Church
  56A St. James Church ~ Watercolor by Clayton Giles
57. St. Philips Church
  57A NHCPL
58. St. John's Episcopal Church
  58A NHCPL ~ *Ballou's Pictorial Drawing-Room Companion*, 26 Sept. 1857
59. Front Street Methodist Church
  59A NHCPL
60. Grace Methodist Church
  60A NHCPL
61. St. Luke's A.M.E. Zion Church
  61A North Carolina Collection ~ UNC-Chapel Hill
62. First Presbyterian Church
  62A NHCPL
63. St. Andrew's Presbyterian Church
  63A Walter Conser
  63B NHCPL ~ *Star-News*
64. Immanuel Presbyterian Church
  64A NHCPL
  64B NHCPL ~ *Star-News*
65. Brooklyn & Calvary Baptist Churches
  65A First Baptist Church
  65B NHCPL

66. First Baptist Church
  66A NHCPL ~ Bill Reaves Collection
67. Shiloh Baptist Church
  67A NHCPL ~ Bill Reaves Collection
68. Mount Nebo Baptist Church
  68A NHCPL ~ Bill Reaves Collection
69. First Advent Christian Church
  69A NHCPL
70. First Church of Christ, Scientist
  70A NHCPL
71. St. Matthew's Lutheran Church
  71A NHCPL
72. Oak Grove Cemetery
  72A NHCPL ~ Louis T. Moore Collection
  72B NHCPL ~ Bill Reaves Collection
73. Oakdale Cemetery
  73A NHCPL
  73B NHCPL
  73C NHCPL
  73D NHCPL
Part Four: Commercial & Office Spaces
  NHCPL
74. Market Street Trade
  74A NHCPL
  74B NHCPL
  74C NHCPL
  74D NHCPL ~ W.B. Creasy Collection
75. Masonic Hall & Carolina Hotel
  75A NHCPL
  75B NHCPL
76. McEachern Feed & Grain Store
  76A NHCPL ~ Gift of Tabitha McEachern
77. The Unlucky Corner
  77A NHCPL ~ Robert M. Fales Collection
78. City Laundry Company
  78A NHCPL
  78B NHCPL ~ Allegood Collection
79. North Front Street
  79A NHCPL
  79B NHCPL
  79C NHCPL
  79D NHCPL
  79E NHCPL
80. Bank of Cape Fear
  80A NHCPL ~ *Ballou's Pictorial Drawing-Room Companion*, 26 Sept. 1857
81. Bank of New Hanover
  81A NHCPL ~ Allegood Collection

133B - *American Country Houses of To-Day*
133B NHCPL - *Star-News*
134. Harbor Island Auditorium
    134A Bellamy Mansion Museum
    134B NHCPL
135. U.S.O Club at Harbor Island
    135A NHCPL
136. Early Lumina
    136A NHCPL
    136B NHCPL
    136C NHCPL
    136D NHCPL
    136E NHCPL
137. Later Lumina
    137A NHCPL
    137B NHCPL
    137C NHCPL
    137D NHCPL ~ *Star-News*
138. Seashore Hotel ~ Ocean Terrace Hotel
    138A NHCPL
    138B NHCPL
    138C NHCPL
139. The Blockade Runner Hotel
    139A NHCPL ~ Photo by Hugh Morton
140. Hotel Tarrymore ~ Oceanic Hotel
    140A NHCPL
    140B NHCPL
    140C NHCPL
141. Hanover Seaside Club
    142A NHCPL
    142B Hanover Seaside Club Archives
    142C NHCPL
143. Johnnie Mercer's Pier
    143A NHCPL
    143B NHCPL
144. Shell Island
    144A John Bahr
    144B NHCPL ~ Photo by Hugh Morton
    144C NHCPL ~ Photo by Sam Bissette
145. Station One at Wrightsville Beach
    145A NHCPL ~ W.B. Creasy Collection
    145B NHCPL ~ Allegood Collection
    145C NHCPL
146. Beach Cottages
    146A NHCPL
    146B NHCPL
    146C NHCPL
    146D NHCPL

147. Beach Inns & Guesthouses
    147A NHCPL
    147B NHCPL ~ Allegood Collection
    147C NHCPL ~ Allegood Collection
    147D NHCPL ~ Bill Reaves Collection
148. Carolina Beach
    148A Elaine Henson
    148B NHCPL
    148C NHCPL
    148D Elaine Henson
    148E NHCPL
    148F Elaine Henson
    148G NHCPL
    148H Elaine Henson
    148I NHCPL
    148J Elaine Henson

Bibliography

Bishir, Catherine W. and Southern, Michael T. *A Guide to the Historic Architecture of Eastern North Carolina.* Chapel Hill, NC: University of North Carolina Press, 1996.

Block, Susan Taylor. *Along the Cape Fear.* Charleston, SC: Arcadia Publishing, 1998.

Block, Susan Taylor. *Cape Fear Beaches*. Charleston, SC: Arcadia Publishing, 2000.

Block, Susan Taylor. *Cape Fear Lost.* Charleston, SC: Arcadia Publishing, 1999.

Block, Susan Taylor. *Wilmington Through The Lens of Louis T. Moore.* Wilmington, NC: Lower Cape Fear Historical Society & New Hanover Public Library, 2001.

Cashman, Diane Cobb. *Cape Fear Adventure, An Illustrated History of Wilmington.* Woodland Hills, CA: Windsor Publications, 1982.

City of Wilmington Illustrated – 1914. Wilmington, NC: Southern Press, 1914.

City of Wilmington, North Carolina, Playground of the South. Wilmington, NC: privately printed, 1920s.

Conser, Walter H. *Sacred Spaces: Architecture and Religion in Historic Wilmington.* Wilmington, NC: Bellamy Mansion Museum of History and Design Arts, 1999.

DeRosset, William Lord. *New Hanover County and Wilmington North Carolina 1723-1938.* Wilmington, NC: privately printed, 1938.

Fales, Robert M. *Wilmington Yesteryear.* Wilmington, NC: privately printed, 1984.

Hall, Lewis Philip. *Land of the Golden River*, volume One, *Old Times on the Seacoast, 1526 to 1970.* Wilmington, NC: privately printed, 1975.

Hall, Lewis Philip. *Land of the Golden River*, volume Two, *This Fair Land of Ours* and volume Three, *Old Wilmington and the Greater in its March to the Sea,* (Two and Three in one volume), Wilmington, NC: privately printed, 1980.

Hewlett, Crockette W. and Smalley, Mona. *Between The Creeks, Masonboro Sound, 1735-1985.* Wilmington, NC: privately printed, 1985.

Howe, Samuel. *American Country Houses of To-Day.* New York; The Architectural Book Publishing Company, 1915.

Hutteman, Ann Hewlett. *Wilmington North Carolina: A Postcard History.* Charleston, SC: Arcadia Publishing, 2000.

Kernon, Charles R. *Rails To Weeds: Searching Out the Ghost Railroads Around Wilmington.* Wilmington, NC: privately printed, 1988 and 1995.

Koeppel, Andrew. *Wilmington Then and Now.* Wilmington, NC: privately printed, 1999.

MacMillan, Emma Woodard. *Wilmington's Vanished Homes and Buildings.* Raleigh, NC: privately printed, 1966.

Mercantile and Industrial Review of Wilmington, New Hanover County, North Carolina. Seaboard Air Line Railway. Portsmouth, VA: privately printed, 1908.

McKoy, Henry Bacon. *Wilmington, N.C. – Do You Remember When?* Greenville, SC: privately printed, 1957.

Reaves Collection – Block Files, Subject Files and Family Files. New Hanover County Public Library.

Turberg, Edward F. and Martin, Christopher. *Historic Architecture of New Hanover County, North Carolina.* Wilmington, NC: New Hanover County Planning Department, 1986.

New Hanover County, The Sub-Tropical Region of the Old North State. Wilmington Chamber of Commerce. Wilmington, NC: privately printed, 1896.

Souvenir of Wilmington, North Carolina. Wilmington, NC: privately printed, 1902.

Reaves, William M. *"Strength Through Struggle" The Chronological and Historical Record of the African-American Community in Wilmington, North Carolina, 1865-1950.* Wilmington, NC: New Hanover Public Library, 1998.

Reilly, J.S. *Wilmington, Past, Present & Future.* Wilmington, NC: privately printed, 1884.

Russell, Anne. *Wilmington, A Pictorial History.* Virginia Beach, VA: The Doning Company, 1981.

Watkins, Greg and the Wrightsville Beach Preservation Society. *Wrightsville Beach, A Pictorial History.* Virginia Beach, VA: The Donning Company, 1997.

Watson, Alan D. *Wilmington, North Carolina, to 1861.* Jefferson, NC: McFarland & Company, 2003.

Wilmington, The Metropolis and Port of North Carolina, Its Advantages and Interests. Wilmington Chamber of Commerce. Wilmington, NC: privately printed, 1912.

Wilmington Up-To-Date, The Metropolis of North Carolina Graphically Portrayed. Wilmington Chamber of Commerce. Wilmington, NC: privately printed, 1902.

Wrenn, Tony P. *Wilmington, North Carolina, An Architectural and Historical Portrait.* Charlottesville, VA: University of Virginia Press, 1984.

Index

About the Author...

Beverly Tetterton is a research librarian in the North Carolina Room at the New Hanover County Public Library. She is a long time volunteer at the Historic Wilmington Foundation where she chairs the historic plaque committee. She served on Wilmington's Historic District Commission for a decade. Her interests include historic preservation, local history, family history and architectural history. In 2001, the Raleigh *News & Observer* named her Tar Heel of the Week. She and her husband, Glenn, co-authored the *North Carolina County Fact Book*. They live in Wilmington's Historic District.

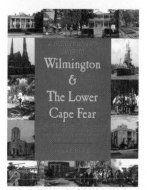
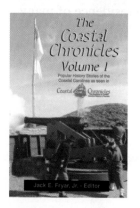

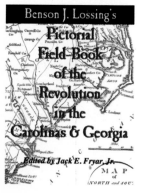

Chronicles of the Cape Fear River: 1660 - 1916 by James Sprunt
(ISBN 0-9723240-5-4 • $34.95) Blockade runner, philanthopist, business man and historian - James Sprunt was all of that and more. He once owned the famous Orton Plantation and Wilmington's Dudley Mansion. His family cotton business was the largest exporter of the fiber in the world. He was also a life-long lover of the Cape Fear. This book is Sprunt's signature history of the place that he loved more than any other. Originally published in 1918, it is still the yardstick by which all other histories of the Cape Fear are measured. If you love the Cape Fear and North Carolina's history, then you absolutely must have this unique and all-encompassing history of the region!

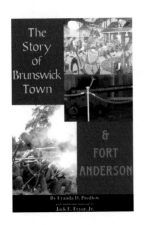

The Story of Brunswick Town & Fort Anderson by Franda D. Pedlow and Jack E. Fryar, Jr. (ISBN 0-9723240-6-2 • $12.95) In 1725, Maurice Moore and his brothers began selling plots of land in Brunswick, the first permanent port on the Cape Fear. It was raided by Spanish privateers, burned and looted by the British in the Revolutionary War, was home to two of North Carolina's Royal Governors, and the residence of many of the Cape Fear's most prominent founding fathers and mothers. In the Civil War, the ruins were chosen as the site of Fort Anderson, the massive earthen fort that was the last installation guarding the Confederacy's vital port at Wilmington. This is the story of Brunswick and Fort Anderson and the state historic site that now preserves their memories.

Rebel Gibraltar: Fort Fisher and Wilmington, C.S.A. by James L. Walker, Jr. (ISBN 0-9723240-7-0 • $30.00) Called the "Gibraltar of the South," Fort Fisher was the huge earthen fortification that was the linchpin of the Cape Fear defense system in the Civil War. While other books have done excellent jobs of telling the story of the capture of Fort Fisher and Wilmington, James L. Walker, Jr.'s book is the first to cover the fort and the city it protected over the course of the entire war. Copiously illustrated with period photographs and maps by noted mapmaker Mark A. Moore, this is the story of the men in gray who slugged it out on the Cape Fear beaches to protect the lifeblood of the Confederacy coming in on swift and daring blockade runners, and their ultimate defeat in 1865.

To Order:

• *Send check or money order to us at:*

Dram Tree Books
549 Eagle Lane
Southport, N.C. 28461

• *Enclose the purchase price for each book, plus $4.00 shipping for the first book, and $1.00 for each additional book.*
• *Please allow two weeks for delivery.*
(910) 538-4076

dramtreebooks@ec.rr.com

Dram Tree
Books
A JEF Publications Company